S0-BDP-407

Producing BRILLIANT Children

Producing BR★iLLIANT Children

JEAN LLOYD, PH.D.

 VANTAGE PRESS

Cover design by Molly Morgan
Text design by Maria E. Torres, Neuwirth & Associates, Inc.
Vantage Press and the Vantage Press colophon
are registered trademarks of Vantage Press, Inc.

FIRST EDITION

All rights reserved, including the right of
reproduction in whole or in part in any form.

Copyright © 2012 by Jean Lloyd, Ph.D.
Published by Vantage Press, Inc.

419 Park Ave. South, New York, NY 10016

Manufactured in the United States of America
ISBN: 978-0-533-16423-3

Library of Congress Catalog Card No: 2011913932

0 9 8 7 6 5 4 3 2 1

To my grandmother, Lula Brown; my mother,
Gladys Lloyd, and my daughter, Jamie Lloyd, who contributed to
this project in many ways.

Also, to the children of P.S. 68 (Man.), P.S. 207/149 (Man.)
and P.S. 108 (Bronx)

Also, to Dr. Lloyd Barenblatt, my mentor at
New York University.

LuZ Borrero 2003 K-1
this story is about SOMETHING Beautiful
the girl Passed a dark alley—No
flowers only trash. she pLanted
flowers. She felt powerfuL.

CONTENTS

WHY I AM WRITING THIS BOOK

PRODUCING BRILLIANT CHILDREN is conceived as a "how-to" book, meant to inspire a new generation of beginning or inexperienced teachers. It is a day-to-day, minute-to-minute, step-by-step guide and manual that takes a teacher through the curriculum. I have modeled it on the extraordinary books of Sylvia Ashton-Warner, that quirky and wonderfully creative teacher, who was able to educate Maori children, a disadvantaged and indigenous group, both racially and culturally different from the European settlers in New Zealand. She used cultural forms familiar to her children to propel them into reading and writing. She let them write about the ghosts that troubled their dreams and discuss household problems that European children would normally have been discouraged from divulging. She understood that building on their interests would help to "plug" them into European modes of learning that they would need to succeed academically. Believe me, in the 1950s this was innovative and daring.

I love her approach—part storytelling, part autobiography and partly an Educational Methods course for teachers. Those methods scandalized her contemporaries and I remember one New Zealand educator telling me, with eyebrows raised, that Ashton-Warner was "dotty" and she drank. Nevertheless, I have borrowed some aspects of her style and approach. After forty-three years of teaching, in kindergarten and university, I recognize the brilliance and originality of her work and remained mindful of it as I did my thesis work. Please note this discussion in the piece called "What Sylvia Ashton-Warner Taught Me."

In this book, I propose a whole curriculum that seeks to develop the brilliant children I taught in Harlem and produce scholarly, well-rounded students. My program, which stresses intrinsic intellectual motivation or "love of learning," correlates highly with outstanding academic achievement, as my thesis shows.

First of all, I need a whole year with my pupils. This is not an intervention where one meets with kids a few times a week. The teacher must be in the classroom daily, must know the progress of each child (the strengths and weaknesses) so that as the child gains in awareness, has an "Aha moment," the teacher can note it, then build on it.

The teacher must have a mission. Mine has been to teach reading and writing (together). But I can best accomplish this if I can motivate them to "love to learn." I think of teaching as both an art and a science, so a pedagogic structure must exist but aesthetic appreciations must also be developed.

Here are some of my procedures that encourage "love of learning."

☆ The Storytime occurs on the rug. Let the children cluster close to the teacher, legs crossed, eyes on the teacher in a figurative grandmotherly embrace.

☆ For the first three months, never read a book to the class that you, the teacher, don't love. They will absorb the pleasure that you feel. You need to love the story, pictures, the way the story is told.

☆ For at least two months, don't ask questions at the end of the book or story. Draw them in! Enchant them! Pelt them with stories! Overwhelm them! The questions can come later. First you must weave a spell.

☆ Storybooks must be really beautiful with gorgeous primary colors, or really artistic and skillfully drawn. For example, a book like *Mufaro's Beautiful Daughters* is a work of art.

☆ Let them create their own books as soon as possible. Early in the year, I organize the pages and then write down the words that the child gives me, while he/she draws the pictures. As we talk about pets, trips, activities at home, I can offer the child several story lines.

☆ We will move from class stories to chart paper to class storybooks. After every event (i.e. a class trip) a book is produced. Early in the year each child gets a page in our group storybook, where I will write their comments while they draw the picture. They may choose to copy their comments from chart paper stories. Soon enough as their phonic skills grow they will want to write their own thoughts as well as illustrate their books.

☆ Be prepared to waste reams of paper and markers. There will be accidents and corrections as we get clean copy. When the children realize that only correct work is displayed or shown to the principal, they accept the challenge.

☆ Our class is required to produce at least one bulletin board monthly. The early writers and readers get the chance to create their own bulletin boards. One child can write the story and another can draw the pictures. I always have children who can do the story *and* pictures. At the end of such a project, photos are taken and parents are invited to see the artistic results.

☆ We have had much success with talented children who delight in reading their books to other classes, to visitors. This in turn motivates their classmates.

☆ Friday is a performance day. In the morning I am testing. Afternoons are devoted to movies, kids who read to the class, popcorn.

PROLOGUE

IT WAS EIGHT O'CLOCK in the evening after a grueling first day in my Harlem school. The kids had been fine. After all, there were only twelve so far—adorable fours and fives in the school uniform of either light blue shirts and navy pants or neat plaid jumpers. The little girls seemed very mature as they whispered and giggled, their hairdos laced with beads or coaxed into fat pom-poms. Some had tiny hoops in their ears and some had pale pink nails. They huddled in small groups on the meeting rug and quietly chattered, even when I was talking. The boys talked to each other but some were already crawling over to look in the bins on the shelves and touch the blocks and cars and traffic signs. The grueling part had been emptying box after box of books, desk supplies, dolls, rolls of paper, and piles of pictures for my eight bulletin boards. Lots of pictures and bright colors are de rigueur these days to give the impression that the kindergarten classroom is a cheerful place where learning is pleasant. Lots of us "early childhood people" now go to teachers' stores where we spend big bucks on colorful borders to frame our bulletin boards and large and small cutouts of days of the week, number patterns, months of the year, and seasons. You can get brightly colored groupings of grammatical parts of speech, famous African Americans, or holiday activities. Commercial decoration is "in" and although I value attractive, planned spaces, my generation of senior teachers was taught that store-bought materials were tacky and teacher-made materials were always better, cheaper, and more professional.

My sister
Tanisha
9/91

As a dazzling pink-gold sunset colored the room, I was now ready for my "first day" ritual, an activity which told me a tremendous amount about my new students. I knew that the year would be full of surprises, reversals, and disappointments, but I was willing to bet that right now, on the first day, I could begin to see that nucleus of talent, stars that would race ahead of the others academically, leading the way. Brighter children might come later and slower children might suddenly take off intellectually, like Roman candles, but right now I could make a few pretty accurate predictions. I opened a folder which contained crayon drawings; I had asked my kindergarteners to draw a picture about their summer vacation. Some tried to draw Disney World, Mount Morris Park, their brothers and sisters. Since they are mainly five-year-olds, their ability to draw is limited. A person is represented as a circle with two sticks for legs. My job, during this arts lesson, is to circulate and ask questions about what they are doing. Generally, I write what they tell me right on the drawing and even have a class conference where they share what they have done. However, at night and alone, I scrutinized my little harvest. Among the squiggles, there were balls, a rainbow, more squiggles, a lot of suns, a blob that was supposed to be a dinosaur and a lot of unrecognizable stuff. But three were worth more attention.

Kenya, one of my "little old ladies," had made a picture of her grandmother. Instead of a one-inch circle, with sticks for legs, grandmother took up the whole eight-by-ten paper. Her head was four inches across and the swirls of curly hair added two inches on each side. She had eyes, eyebrows, and a big smile. Although she was shaped like a large egg, the stumps at her side were obviously arms, and the straight lines were fingers. Kenya had written her own name using capital and lowercase letters. A picture like this tells me a lot about this child's ability to think spatially, also to see details (Grandmother had eyes with pupils and eyelashes.). Noticing and remembering details is crucial in reading and this sweet child had come to school already aware of details of anatomy. In addition, she was proficient in the first skill we would have to teach—writing her name in upper and lowercase letters. Hallelu-jah! While some children need a vacation period like the Easter holidays to digest ideas and concepts before things fall into place and suddenly they are reading, others like Kenya begin much earlier. They come to school with a repertoire of skills, so they sit and watch me teaching with their eyes dancing. You can see that they understand and, in fact, they are having a good time.

The second drawing was completely different. Crystal, a child so wound-up that she spent periods of time whirling around and around, had produced a tiny figure, again with face, hair, arms, a torso, and legs in pants. All around were phrases and letters of the alphabet. Except for the word *hello* all of the letters were capitalized. When I saw "WE WILL HAVE . . ." I realized that she had been copying words from the bulletin boards. Her printing was neat, well formed and what I would expect at the end of the school year. I made a mental note to find out if there was an older sibling or a helpful parent giving her attention and skills. Very promising!

The third drawing was produced by a boy. It was a picture of Pokemon. Rather than ask, "What is that?" a question that makes some children defensive, I asked instead, "Is it something special?" He told me that Pokemon was a dragon. His drawing showed skill. There were anatomical details, and he had written the word *Poke-mon* under his picture. I know very little about this new media sensation, a focus of much shopping and television viewing, but I recognized the maturity of the drawing and its presentation and immediately became interested in the child.

Reflection on these pictures reminded me of my first class in this Harlem school in 1990. I remembered a ragged little five-year-old named Alicia. My experience with this child illustrated all the problems to be found in ghetto schools, but also the rich-ness and promise within them. I had been hired after the term had begun because there had been a bumper crop of five-year-olds that year. Because black parents are very concerned with the physical appearance of their children and there is much braiding of hair as well as buying of clothes that reflect adult fashion trends, little

Alicia stood out. She was scraggly and unkempt and cross-eyed. She wore sandals, dirty little cotton dresses without a slip and one day she came without underpants. She occasionally smelled of urine. It was sobering to watch the other children as we sat on the rug during morning meeting. They delicately sniffed the air, unsure where the smell was located. During such times Alicia sat, watching me intently, absorbed by the lesson, a half-smile on her face. The reactions of her classmates didn't seem to bother her. After all, she was quick to punch any child who annoyed her.

I clearly remember the day when I realized that she was special. I had been given a set of ancient, yellowing workbooks to use as teaching aids. Although I was used to more current and attractive reading materials, they were adequate because they provided instruction in phonics. If the children could learn the sounds of all the alphabet letters, they were well on their way in reading. There is a magic that happens when they understand that printed words are made up of alphabet sounds. Anyway, I taught my first lesson in my new kindergarten using the letter *b*. We made the sound, then looked at boats, books, bells, and bicycles focusing on the first sound. This is not easy stuff for disadvantaged children like mine because they may not see the importance of sounds, or words. They may have little experience with print because no one reads stories to them or allows them to handle picture books with words. Worse yet, some parents do not talk to their children at all. They may give them directions but have not learned the gentle art of conversing with them and exchanging opinions and communicating sources of pleasure. It was clear to me that I would have to repeat the phonics lesson several times in different guises until they made the connection between the letter and the sound. The next day I held up a picture of a boat. When I asked, "What is the first sound in 'boat'?" Alicia made the *b* sound, loud and clear. I was frankly astonished and delighted. In the days that followed, she learned and remembered each sound.

That same year, a group of researchers came to our school from Columbia University, intent on learning more about a largely unknown population, gifted minority children. They tested all of the five-year-olds and they confirmed my suspicions about Alicia. She was a brilliant child. In 1993, The U.S. Department of Education issued a report, *National Excellence: A Case for Developing America's Talent.* (Washington, DC) They described Alicia in a sidebar that charted her progress in a summer program at the Teachers College. In spite of being one of eleven children under age thirteen, in spite of a crack-addicted mother and absentee father, she showed sophisticated abilities in mathematics, testing at the 85th percentile on a standardized math assessment. She could then concoct imaginative stories and was teaching herself to read more fluently. At the end of elementary school, she was accepted into a gifted program for middle school children.

The point is that I encounter children like Alicia all the time. The kindergarten years are that golden time when little children run into the classroom each morning bubbling with excitement. School is a daily adventure and teachers are like wizards, full of secrets and surprises. At this age there are many Alicias, in suburban as well as in ghetto schools like mine.

I had come to my school, P.S. 207, in 1990. It is a modern-looking building, connected to another school, P.S. 149, by a corridor that used to house a prekindergarten of four-year-olds and two kindergartens of fives. At present my school is pleasant to look at, with new green casement windows and enlarged drawings from African American picture books actually painted on the outside walls of the building. In addition to doors leading to the hallway, these three classrooms have doors opening onto a charming playground with trees, benches, and space for gardening. Unlike many city school buildings that were built in the first decade of the twentieth century and resemble stone fortresses, my school was constructed in the 1960s. Over the past few years, New York Cares, a group of corporate employees, have devoted time to us so that there are floor-to-ceiling murals in the gyms, lunchrooms, and on the upper grade playground. There is no crumbling brick or peeling paint and the corridors on the first floor are waxed each day after the children leave. Charming setting . . . big problems.

1

How I Begin—Memorization—
A Technique to Build Vocabulary and
Repertoire—Acquiring Cultural Capital

WHEN I WAS YOUNG, we had to memorize "pieces" for special occasions. No one asked if you wanted to. You just did. The first time that I can remember memorizing anything of significance was in a program in church when I was seven years old. At P.S. 54, my elementary school in Brooklyn, we were memorizing all the time because there were weekly assemblies with songs and choral speaking. In time we had learned a store of songs and poems that became part of our repertoire of "cultural capital." What a different world! They moved the walls, not the children. By pushing the sliding doors that separated the classrooms, we remained at our desks and the whole floor of classrooms took part and sang. At P.S. 54 the teachers were Irish, very old, with snow white hair or wigs, especially drawn to folk music from the old country. I, an African American child, could sing all the verses of "The Minstrel Boy to the War Has Gone," "Cockles and Mussels," and "When Irish Eyes Are Smiling." Even now, I can sing the Italian medley that we learned. "Santa Lucia" was my favorite. And unhappily, as my brother and I were the only black children in the school, every year in honor of

Black History Week, the whole assembly sang the spiritual, "Let My People Go" while looking at us . . . and they sang it very slowly. I kept my head down and did the closest thing to blushing that I was capable of.

But my first standup recitation was Clement Moore's "The Night Before Christmas." (1936) My Sunday school teacher decided that I could do it in the Christmas show and after my mother was consulted, a printed copy was given to me. Typically, no one asked me if I wanted to and because I had never recited before, I gritted my teeth and saw it as a new trial to be endured. At seven, there were few things that grown-ups required, that one really wanted to do (i.e., eating hot cereal or getting one's hair braided or making beds).

The Christmas program was to be held in the First African Methodist Episcopal Zion Church of Brooklyn, where my parents were members. They rarely attended, but my brother and I had to go, both to Sunday school and church, weekly. The church was so far away we were each given two nickels for the trolley, together with a promise that we could go to the movies in the afternoon. We habitually walked home, so one nickel bought an ice-cream cone or a candy bar. The long walk home simply provided my parents with more private time together, so they never asked why we were late.

Once I had been given the poem to learn, it became my responsibility. I don't remember getting any help or encouragement. Southern black parents of that era didn't coddle their children. They didn't negotiate with them and they didn't give them choices. They gave you orders—not loudly or in anger; they were matter of fact. But you were expected to obey.

Therefore I read the poem over and over and began to remember it, line by line. Sometimes the language baffled me. "More rapid than eagles his coursers they came." What were "coursers?" Apparently I didn't have to understand it, just memorize it. I had had my library card from an early age, so I was a competent reader but the poem was full of things I didn't understand. "And mamma in her kerchief, and I in my cap, had just settled our brains for a long winter's nap . . ." Why were they wearing headgear in bed? And why was Santa Claus described as little? ". . . A miniature sleigh and eight tiny reindeer . . ." At that time I still believed in Santa Claus, but I thought that he was at least a big as my father.

Toward the end of the week, I had most of it memorized. But could I remember it all? There must have been rehearsals, but I have retained no memory of them. By Saturday, my mother asked me if I were ready. She seemed calm. She was probably remembering my feat of an earlier time. The Sunday school teacher had offered a prize to the child who could recite the Ten Commandments. I won, having learned them over the weekend (as written) but scandalized her by refusing the first prize (a pair of slippers) and demanding the second prize (a bottle of bubble bath). I was thrilled with that bubble bath, knowing that my parents would never give me so frivolous a gift. The Ten Commandments had been a challenge that *I* had chosen, taking a certain pleasure in rattling them off to the dismay of my classmates. But the Christmas poem was different. I was doing it because *they* wanted me to. Waiting to perform became agonizing. *Why had they done this to me?* I wondered. *What if I forget a line or phrase? It would embarrass my parents.* I did not dare to forget.

The day of the show, I wandered around the house feeling cold. At the church, I sat in the audience, very still and cold, hearing voices buzzing around me but unable to respond. I must have rehearsed with my Sunday school teacher, but I don't remember doing so. I do remember walking up onto the stage, utterly alone. I was numbed by the silence. Floating before me were hundreds of eyes. A seven-year-old child.

" 'Twas the night before Christmas and all through the house . . ." After the first sentence the rest came easily. The poem had become part of me. On automatic pilot, it flowed on and on, just as I had rehearsed it . . . slow, loud, measured, with expression. Not a word was forgotten. I did not leave out any lines. The narrative carried me. I expected to have trouble with the description of Santa because I had difficulty thinking of him as a "jolly old elf." And I usually got stuck on "His droll little mouth was drawn up like a bow." But by the time I got to his little "round belly" and "a bowl full of jelly," I knew that I could finish it, so I coasted to the end. There was much applause when I finished but there was no joy in it. Only relief. My parents were pleased but they didn't make a fuss about it. We went home and that was that.

My experience at church taught me several important things. Just as I had found with subjects I disliked, success was often achieved after torment . . . not anxiety or discomfort . . . but agony and torment. With highly strung, extremely shy people like me, there would always be a price to be paid for extended effort that led to some precious goal. I would relate it to the situation of some actors who throw up and get sick before a performance. I have read that the great tenor Franco Corelli of Metropolitan Opera fame eventually retired because the pain before a performance never lessened; the agony was so great, he reached a point where enough was enough. (Franco Corelli, "Italian Tenor of Power and Charisma, and Pillar of the Met, Dies at 82," *New York Times*, October 30, 2003, C14)

At seven, I realized that I could achieve things. I could triumph, as it were. And even though my performance in church had left me relieved, but drained, in time performance would bring me elation, a dizzy high that would have me remembering my moments on stage with secret smiles and inner joy. In time I would become aware of the power that a performer has, to beguile an audience, to hold them suspended by enchantments that could be woven with words.

However, as a young person I was confronted with periodic "torments." Learning the multiplication table in order to take a test was arduous. Practicing and then performing Chopin's *Polonaise* in a recital at eleven years old, was an experience that I endured. However, later I was extremely proud that I had learned such a difficult piece. Studying for the Graduate Record Examination was nerve-racking because, until I had passed, I could not legitimately enter the doctoral program at New York University. Agony and torment, then success and elation, a thread that runs through life as we move from stage to stage and plateau to plateau. People like me, realizing soon enough that most of life's challenges are accomplished alone, learn to reach deep within to some unknown place to tear success out and force defeat away. So far, it has always been worth the pain.

Years later when I became a teacher, my past experiences shaped my practice. Being able to stand before an audience and present something to them was an invaluable skill. As a teenager I felt a growing ease and self-confidence, sure to make classroom recitations more successful. It became part of a "presentation of self" that would make participation in plays, debates, and platform exercises fun and would later influence career choices (television, teaching) where sophistication in communication was necessary. Most importantly, the things one memorized became part of one's knowledge base, the "cultural capital" that would accompany one through life. I can still recite the soliloquies from Shakespeare that I learned in junior high and they still connect me to a glorious dramatic tradition as well as give me pleasure. Cultural capital consists of the knowledge and accomplishments acquired first in the family setting. Pierre Bourdieu, a sociologist of culture and education, emphasizes that in our capitalist society those children who come to school already competently using the language, symbols, and ideas of the dominant culture will do better academically and be better able to secure favored positions in the job and professional markets. (Sedgwick, 1973, 2002)

To my surprise, I later learned, as a kindergarten teacher, that while seven-year-olds may experience torment in performance, *most four and five-year-olds do not.* Therefore, it makes a lot of sense to get them used to speaking up as soon as possible, reciting, answering questions, making observations in the interest of self-confidence as well as repertoire. So that every September, within the first hour of the first day of school, I teach my kindergarteners their first poem, Vachel Lindsay's "The Little Turtle," (1920) the first of perhaps thirty or forty poems that they will learn. It is the beginning of a love affair with language, written expression and literature that should never end. Let me show you how I begin.

THE FIRST RECITATION

The children are seated on the rug (rugs are obligatory and they used to come out of the teachers' paycheck). I indicate that we are going to have some fun. We cup our hands into a little box and I recite:

> There was a little turtle and he lived in a box.
> (We peek in.)
>
> He swam in the puddles and he climbed on the rocks.
> (Dramatize using hands.)
>
> He snapped at a mosquito; he snapped at a flea.
> (Snapping with one hand.)
>
> He snapped at a minnow; he snapped at me.
>
> He caught the mosquito; he caught the flea.
> (Clap hands together.)
>
> He caught the minnow . . . but he didn't catch me.

This is a "finger play" so it is acted out with much waggling of hands, snapping, and catching. The end is significant because there is a triumphant note. The child touches his or her chest. "He didn't catch me." It is always a huge success and there is much giggling. After explaining that a minnow is a tiny fish, I repeat this poem several times and suggest that the children join in. They always learn it quickly and enjoy the sense of mastery that the last line implies. Finger plays are an integral part of my Language Arts Program.

GOALS FOR SEPTEMBER, OCTOBER, AND NOVEMBER

The first few months of school will be devoted to two major goals. My Board of Education goal, the goal to which I admit in curriculum conferences, is familiar to most kindergarten planners. My first job is to prepare my charges for the rigors of the coming year. Some children have had extensive day care experience. Others have been in the care of neighborhood child care providers. Some have had no group experiences outside the home. Therefore, my first unit of work is called *Getting Started in School*. My children must learn a number of social skills—to walk quickly and quietly, to listen for instructions, to raise hands when seeking the teacher's attention, to hold a partner's hand, to clean up after playtime, solve conflicts rationally, work cooperatively in small groups—all of this while beginning reading, writing, and social studies, geography, music, thinking skills, art, and physical education activities.

However, it is my second goal that anchors my whole educational program. I must make my pupils "love to learn." If they come racing into school each day, eyes shining with excitement, they will be ready to learn the things I have to teach. This "love of learning" will provide the motivation for high intellectual attainment and academic achievement. Because of my research with Dr. Lloyd Barenblatt at New York University, I am now prepared to share an educational philosophy and at the same time share day-to-day activities that encourage early reading ability and a true love of learning, the key to intrinsic intellectual motivation and high academic achievement. These produce brilliant children. (See p. 209 for essay.)

THEMES THAT ARE APPROPRIATE FOR DEVELOPING CURRICULUM
(Themes generally last for two weeks.)
  - ☆ Getting Started in School
  - ☆ Autumn and the Harvest
  - ☆ Halloween (Spooky stories but also discussions of safety while trick-or-treating)
  - ☆ Families (Different family groupings)
  - ☆ Being Healthy (Discuss diet, visit to the dentist, healthy lifestyles
  - ☆ Being Safe (Fire prevention, poisons, drugs)
  - ☆ Dinosaurs (In preparation for our trip to the Museum of Natural History)
  - ☆ The Pilgrims and Thanksgiving

- ☆ Winter Holidays (We study seasonal changes and nonreligious activities relating Christmas and Chanukah—Frosty the Snowman, The Nutcracker)
- ☆ The New Year (Also discuss time—days of the week, months, birthdays)
- ☆ Dr. Martin Luther King's birthday (The Montgomery bus boycott—Rosa Parks—segregation)
- ☆ Groundhog Day
- ☆ President's Day
- ☆ Black History Month (Ruby Bridges, Bessie Coleman, Harriet Tubman)
- ☆ Spring (Seasonal changes)
- ☆ Baby Animals (Preparation for our trip to the zoo)
- ☆ Spring Holidays (The Easter Bunny, spring festivals of ethnic groups)
- ☆ Mammals, insects, reptiles (Start a butterfly garden)
- ☆ Ocean creatures (Visit to the aquarium)
- ☆ Earth Day
- ☆ The Sky (Planetarium visit—the planets, the moon, the sun)
- ☆ Special Projects (i.e., class prepares an assembly program)
- ☆ Summer Safety

2

September . . . the First Day—
Step-by-Step . . .

ON THE FIRST DAY, I must plan carefully and move slowly. My first activity is to get the children from the yard or the lunchroom and walk them back to the classroom safely. On the spot I choose two monitors (children standing quietly waiting for instructions are good candidates). They must hold hands and all the children assembled must partner up. With an assistant to help me or with several teary-eyed parents (apparently experiencing separation anxiety), I must get the children into the building, sometimes up to the second floor. The monitors must learn to hold the doors, then remain at the back of the line until called. I am willing to let crying children walk with Mommy because it is expedient, but I need to get the class moving. At the classroom door, if possible, I send parents on their way. If a child refuses to let Mommy go, the parent joins us (sometimes for the day, sometimes for the week). In the classroom, the children are seated on the rug in a circle and there are a number of name cards scattered on the rug. While the children are looking around at the brightly decorated room, I quickly print names of the newest arrivals. In general, the children are quiet because I am an unknown factor and the kindergarten class-room looks different from a pre-kindergarten: many pictures but a lot of words, sentences, charts. And many, many books.

After introducing myself, we play our first game. The children are asked to "find your name." Believe me, there is never a mad scramble. Some children will have immediate success and will be able to put the name card over their heads using the attached red yarn (the yarn is light and doesn't irritate their necks). Other children will need help, but this is a good way to introduce the first academic task of the year, *learning our names*. We will play this game daily for a week or more, as new children enter the class. Because name cards are also attached to the tables where they sit and are under the coat hooks in their cubbies, recognizing names happens rather effortlessly during the first week. We are almost ready for the Morning Meeting, our first activity of the day. It is a daily occurrence because young children depend upon routines for security. They need to know what is coming next. Also this large group experience (where major learning takes place) will alternate with small group instruction or individualized instruction (one instructor and one child). Kindergarteners need ample opportunity to move around in groups of varying sizes. We must remember that, at this point, they may have short attention spans and are not used to sitting still for long periods. Also the teacher must plan noisy activities like Choice Time to be followed by quiet activities, like story time. Remember, they are only four and five years old.

ROUTINES TO BEGIN THE DAY

Before Morning Meeting children are allowed to chat quietly with each other while I read notices from the office or talk to monitors who come into the room with urgent messages. This is a relaxed time when whispering is encouraged, when my assistant teacher may be comforting a child who is having trouble masking the anxiety that separation from home brings, when I may be writing the "sentence of the day" to be read momentarily or when a child announces some special event that has happened at home "Guess what? We have a new kitten," or "We went to Disney World." I like to begin Morning Meeting with chords on the piano, followed by a song, "Good morning to you," or "We are glad to see you." Like my inspiration, Sylvia Ashton-Warner, the famed New Zealand educator, whose disadvantaged Maori children looked a lot like mine, music (classical, traditional, popular) is an integral part of the school day. This is a good time to practice the Pledge of Allegiance or any of the songs that will be sung in upcoming assemblies. Our cultural capital thus begins to grow.

Next comes *attendance*. I call each child by name and mark both an attendance book (for me) and the computer printout from the office. Children are required to respond in a sentence and say, "I am here." For many, this marks the beginning of a requirement to speak in full sentences. For the child who has difficulty and says, "Me am here" or "I uh here," I will gently correct, possibly saying, "Say it with me . . . I . . . am. . . . here." Where a child is unable to repeat this sentence, it doesn't pay to make a fuss, though I will note children with immature speech patterns, dialects, inability to speak English, or speech problems. Generally, after hearing other children respond correctly and repeatedly, the sentence is learned.

After attendance, I like to swing into another finger play with lots of opportunity for movement. "Open, Shut Them" is a favorite. I say, "All right, fingers in the air."

Open, shut them, Open, shut them, Give a little clap.

Open, shut them, Open, shut them. Lay them in your lap.

Creep them, creep them . . . way up to your chin.

Open wide your little mouth, but do not put them in!

Open, shut them. Open, shut them.

To your shoulders fly.

Then like little birdies let them flutter in the sky.

Falling, falling, almost to the ground.

Quickly pick them up again and whirl them round and round!

Faster . . . faster . . . slower . . . slower . . . faster . . . slower . . .
Clap!

Like all good finger plays, this one involves a lot of action. The last lines can be extended for a long time as the instructor switches from fast to slow, rapidly or with much drama. Also like all good finger plays, the fun results from careful listening and following instructions. Because these skills are crucial in reading readiness, the more finger plays, the better.

COMING TO ATTENTION

Now it is time for another first-day imperative. Because during the first week, there will be line-ups, fire drills, activities with other kindergarteners, it will be very important to get the class's attention. When the loud speaker comes on, the teacher must have absolute silence or information from the office is missed (frequently the children are being addressed directly). So that during morning meeting, we must practice how to come to attention quickly. My favorite method is to sing:

Stop, look, and listen.
Hear what I am saying . . . Freeze!

I tell them to freeze just like statues. Then we practice. They laugh and skip around; they whirl and tumble for about two minutes, then I sing out, "Stop, look, and listen . . ." If I don't like the result, we'll do it again. They need to understand that I want complete silence and frozen movement. This little exercise will be practiced probably at three different points in the first day's activities. But the result is important. Later, on a trip, in the museum bathroom, when I need to do a quick head count, or in the hallway when we are toileting or when the principal comes into my room and needs to speak to me, I must have their attention in order to give them instructions. Over time, the class becomes very proud of their ability to react quickly, and to function as a group, so from the first day their repertoire of skills has begun to grow.

The first few days of school are always half-days, so I must rush and get two important activities completed. My first story time is going to be the beginning of a love affair with books, so it must be carefully orchestrated. Also I must quickly get a sense of the academic skills of my class. It is already about 9:30 a.m., so it is wise to toilet now. Then we will have a good, uninterrupted stretch of time to work. Although we have had toilets inside the classroom in the past, at the moment, the prekindergartens have the amenities because they are younger. Therefore, I teach toileting routines in the hallway. Even if I have an assistant, this is one more learning experience where behavior must be monitored by the teacher. The first months of school set the tone for the whole year, and I believe that a relaxed attitude in September and carelessly taught routines will cause grief and chaos in January when the children are kept inside because of bad weather and they can become restless and rebellious. In developing routines, my teaching style becomes clear to the casual observer. It is somewhere between authoritative and authoritarian. It became that way the year I marched into the principal's office, crossed my arms and said, "I'm pretty fed up right now. I have a total of twenty-seven children and eight of them appear to have no inner control. They fight, swear, are unable to 'delay gratification,' spit, and throw things. Eight of them! The teachers who cover me on preparation periods can't control them. So when I return to my room, it's a shambles. Eight! I'm talking about children whose behavior is so unusually bizarre, I'm beginning to write anecdotal material so they can be evaluated." The principal said "Eight. That seems to be true in every class." Whereupon I walked back to my classroom, understanding that I was on my own. Help would not be forthcoming. Eight uncontrollable children can wreck a classroom and what is worse, terrify their classmates. So on the first day I begin to develop a level of discipline that gives security to all. Even toileting becomes a routine with behaviors to be learned.

LINING UP AND TOILETING

Inside the classroom, we line up in pairs. I call the children using their table numbers. By now the monitors have increasing confidence so when I say, "Monitors to the front," they move into place. I am at the back of the line, holding the hand of anyone who needs my attention, and directly in front of me may be others who need my attention. (It is entirely possible that the line-up may have to be repeated until it is handled with ease and quiet behavior.) When we go into the hallway, I am directing, "Monitors, walk to the clock and stop." I am also praising. "Good job, class!" We proceed very slowly, with frequent stops. Passing teachers can be very helpful when they comment, "What a lovely class!"

Our bathrooms are side-by-side so that boys and girls separate and form single lines at the doors. They go in two at a time. While they are waiting to enter, I point to bulletin board work outside classrooms. It is important for them to see excellent work, to note seasonal themes, to be aware of interesting class trips that others have made. They may whisper, but we stress the fact that children in surrounding classes are working and we must not disturb them. Children who are finished toileting and washing their hands create a new line, but those who cause disturbances must use the bathroom singly. And I have been known to enter either bathroom to discourage those who stuff rolls of toilet paper down commodes, who start fights when unobserved, or who engage in sex play, acting out what has been observed or experienced. Antisocial behavior is curtailed and diverted but sexual activities get written up and reported to the guidance counselor.

During toileting time, if alone, I must be aware of what is happening in the hallway and in the bathroom, maintain decorum and do a little teaching, too. It is all possible if I can speed things up, maintain an outward calm and watch out for disruptions. Trouble-some children stay near me at all times and may have to endure a "Time out," back in class. If I am lucky enough to have an educa-tional assistant, after perhaps two weeks of having two teachers walking the class to the bathroom, the ed assistant can take small groups alone (not boys, then girls as teachers are now discouraged from unnecessary same-sex distinctions; we call them by tables to line up). The walk back to the classroom is unhurried, with fre-quent stops, praise and comments like, "Eyes in front," "This is not talking time," and "Let's hurry . . . I have the most wonderful story to tell you. It's about billy goats. . . ."

Kindergarten teachers most important *long-term* goals are to teach:

1. *socialization skills*—the internalization of the norms and values important to school success (i.e., perseverance, adequate preparation, good attendance, respect for others, acceptable behavior)
2. *academic skills*—in kindergarten this means to teach the class to read and write well. Added to these are the curricu-lum areas (i.e., math, social studies, geography). The moti-vational tool that animates and excites the student so that the school experience is successful is "a love of learning." I call this *intrinsic intellectual motivation*.

In disadvantaged neighborhoods where students are not meeting the academic standards set by state departments of education, the prekindergarten and kindergarten years are crucial. Because small children learn with such ease, because they can be motivated so easily, also because in later years they may be exposed to uncertified teachers, who may have insufficient skills, I believe that the basic skills can be learned in kindergarten. In 1960, Jerome Bruner, an influential educator at Harvard University, made a statement that is still dear to my heart. He said, "We begin with the hypothesis that any subject can be taught effectively in some intellectually honest form to any child at any stage of development." (*The Process of Education*, 1963) But two things are clear. The teacher who wants to impart knowledge must understand that at any particular age, the subject matter must be presented "in terms of the child's way of viewing things," or presented using language and examples familiar to the child. I have frequently said that it is possible to teach kindergarteners many of the principles of physics using the levers, slides and ramps of the block corner. Also these early learnings can be built upon and extended later into more powerful representations, precisely because they have been understood in the context of play and exploration at an earlier time.

Story Time

As the children hurry back to the classroom, I visibly relax. Story time is like an emotional "coffee break" for me. Whereas, at other times of the day, when I am teaching a skill, with my lesson plan nearby; whereas, I am so aware of connecting ideas I frequently write dialogue in my lesson plan, (the exact words I expect to say) so that I can lead the class to the next level of understanding, at story time . . . we simply enjoy. Many years ago, I was the storyteller at the Hans Christian Andersen statue in New York's Central Park. Nothing gives me the pleasure than telling a story can. We can fly, imaginatively, to other lands, to earlier centuries where everything is mysterious, or dazzling or wrenching. My children get a chance to enter someone else's life to see how they deal with tragedy or pain or sudden wealth or wonderful surprises. Although they are following the pictures, I am painting pictures with the words. At story time we open the great treasure chest that is the English language and begin to feel its power to hold us, to captivate us, to enrich our understandings so that we are wiser, more sensitive, more capable people.

On the first day of school, I choose my first story carefully. The journey begins now. I need the children to begin to love stories so much that story time is one of their favorite times of the day. I want them to be "in love with words" and fascinated with their possibilities. So the first story must be simple in structure, with lots of repetition, so that they can say the words, too. I like stories with drama so that I can become the characters. I will choose a medium sized book to begin with. Although the curriculum is closely related to the "big books" that form our "basic literacy" program, I like to use books of many sizes. After all, some of my favorite books for story hour are not "big books" but if they are presented properly in the right setting, they do the job. For the past few years, I have been using, *The Three Billy Goats Gruff.* (1998) It is not long. It has a wicked troll and lots of repetition so the children can join in.

During story time the children are expected to sit on the rug, with legs crossed and hands in their laps. While they are settling down, I may do a finger play. However, once I begin, there is no talking or touching neighbors. They are encouraged to repeat lines like, "'Who's that trip-tropping across my bridge?' said the troll." And at the very end, we use our fingers like scissors and say, "Snip, snap, snout . . . this tale's told out." At the beginning of the year, I may tell three or four short stories in one sitting. I do not ask questions at this time because I have to give the magic time to work. The stories that the children seem to love will be repeated over and over. In a month, I begin to encourage analysis of story content.

The morning is almost finished. We must get to the writing/drawing piece. So after either a song (e.g., "Skip to My Lou") or another finger play, we will begin a discussion about summer vacation. I may ask, "Who went on a trip?" "What did you see?" "Who went to the park?" "Who played outside on the sidewalk?" "What games did you play?" "I want you to draw a picture that shows what you did." I will give out crayons and paper and as they work, wander around and offer to write what the picture is about. It will be worthwhile to allow a big block of time for this activity. They may do several pictures and I will make sure that I chat with each child. At the end of this time, we will end with a "sharing." Children will be encouraged to show their pictures and tell about them. We will solemnly applaud each presentation and the teacher will say, "Excellent work." "Good job!"

If time has galloped by and we must leave, there are still papers to send home. It is important to give parents an overview of the year, my expectations and their responsibilities. Also, this is a good time to ask for supplies. There are never enough crayons after summer vacation or tissues for runny noses or paper towels for cleanup time. It is crucial to get parent telephone numbers, at work and home and the telephone of a nearby relative in case of emergencies. On the first day, I send home a card asking permission for neighborhood trips. If a child has occasional "accidents" I need an extra set of clothing.

The deluge of paper allows me to obscure the fact that I don't intend to give their drawings back . . . yet. (Remember, my first-day ritual of uncovering "strengths.") Where children insist and want to show Mommy, I dig through the pile. Since they have usually done two or three drawings, there is something to take home. In addition to my nighttime evaluation, tomorrow I will have material for a bulletin board called How I Spent My Summer Vacation. As we admire their first efforts (always one picture for each child), I will compliment the children for some attribute—being able to write their names, ability in drawing, coloring, covering the whole page rather than squeezing everything into a corner. And it will all pay off too. During the next few days I will see them stopping to find their picture and also comparing what they have done with others. Wordlessly, standards begin to be absorbed.

REFLECTIONS ABOUT MY CRAFT . . .

When I returned to Harlem, after teaching in a lovely Bronx school that was called "the country club" by staff in the district office, I resolved that my personal mission was going to be that one thing— I was going to teach reading in kindergarten. (This was well before "the standards.") A number of things strengthened my resolve. It didn't take long to realize that, academically, my new school was a disaster area. When I was able to locate a printout of the citywide reading scores, I thought I was reading a misprint. The statistics showed that fourteen percent of my school's students were reading on grade level. Good grief! That meant that eighty-six percent of them were not. (*New York Times*, February 20, 1993, L22.) Part of the reason for this was the fact that the turnover in faculty was appalling. A parade of young teachers would arrive, get married and apparently need to join their spouses in other states. If they were new teachers and lacked strong classroom management skills and had yet to internalize the elements of a curriculum (meaning that when you walked into the class in September, you already had the year's curriculum in your head and you knew exactly what you would be doing in March) . . . they were in for a rocky ride. Most of the children were manageable but a large number were out of control. The level of aggression, (the fistfights, the cursing, the enraged children, who would knock over chairs, throw things at the teacher and, indeed, hit the teacher) had to be frightening to young people who had gone to stable middle-class schools. Getting married and moving on was one way of getting out. There were always some who quit before September was over, but for the ones who had lasted and gotten tenure, taking tests and becoming guidance counselors or administrators or staff developers was another way out of the classroom.

Having already logged sixteen years in elementary school and a substantial number in college teaching, it was clear to me that a school could sustain a few new teachers from time to time but the wholesale flight of teachers meant a revolving staff of beginners who would not have the stable climate in which to develop the craft and the art of teaching. I resolved to share my skills and experience in my new school. Little did I realize how difficult this would be.

Teachers like Me

And then there are the ones like me, who hate administration and assistant principals because we dislike anyone telling us what to do. We realize that teaching skills can be learned, but we are "born teachers." We come into the classroom and find it to be a stage where we can act out natural inclinations to lead, direct, and guide. We are "prima donnas" and often ignore our own lesson plans because suddenly we want to follow a line of thought with the class that we suspect will yield new understandings. Sometimes we want to "take a flyer" and try something new, guided only by a gut feeling or perhaps bored by the math lesson that is coming or realizing that we have the class at the point where the kids are feeling and understanding and absorbing important ideas. Sometimes you can see by their eyes that they have actually been touched by the majesty of a poetic phrase or they understand the dilemma of a character who needs to make a just and fair decision. Then as a teacher, you are shaping a personality and enlarging a child's vision of what his or her role in the world could be. As a teacher, I make a difference every day. I have the power to enrich other lives, to reveal the excitement of my experiences and my intellectual journeys so that others can be touched by them. It is amazing. I can dream worlds and then cause others to see them. I feel continually blessed.

Sharing Plans with Parents

I jump into reading and writing immediately. These days, even in disadvantaged communities, most children have had some day care or prekindergarten experience; they come to me with an orientation to literacy. They see their brothers and sisters doing homework. They watch their parents fill out forms. On television, there are words and sentences on the screen. In school, from the very beginning, they realize that reading and writing is something that the teacher feels is important. Parents have communicated expectations for their children when on the first day of school I find composition books and pencils in their brand-new book bags. I am always touched when eager parents meet them after the first class and ask about their homework. That very day, I give or send a letter of welcome, a statement about my intentions for the year and my request for classroom supplies. The letter is as follows:

Dear Parents:

We welcome you to our wonderful class. We expect a productive year in Kindergarten. I can promise you that in June your child will be able to read and write well. The following requests and suggestions will prove helpful to you, your child and the teacher:

1. If you have any messages for the teacher, please send written notes. Oral messages carried by the children are often forgotten or misunderstood.
2. If your child is absent, please send a note when he/she returns to school.
3. Please sign and return all forms and notices promptly. Check your child's book bag daily for messages or notices.
4. Please toilet your child just before leaving for school.
5. Our school day starts promptly at 8:30 a.m.
6. If you have not signed a lunch form, one will be sent to you.
7. Kindergarten children are dismissed at 3:00 p.m.
8. When you purchase sweaters, coats or jackets, please be sure that buttons are large enough and zippers are manageable so that the child can achieve independence in dressing. In the case of boots, please buy them large enough for the children to manage themselves.
9. Please send the following items:
   - A pair of scissors (children's safety)
   - A box of large-sized crayons
   - One small Elmer's glue
   - One large box of facial tissues
   - One roll of paper towels
   - Two black and white composition books
   - At least two pencils
   - One book bag

   I always include a request for a year's subscription to a weekly children's magazine like the *Weekly Reader* or *Time For Kids*.
10. If you are available for class trips, let me know.
11. A week from now, you will receive notice of a parents' meeting, inside our classroom. At this time we will explain how we will use the materials in the room for the children's academic development.

With your help, they will be reading and writing quite well by June of next year. We will demonstrate the manipulatives, books, and other learning materials that we use on a daily basis. Please plan to attend our "welcome breakfast" with your child and then come to the parents' meeting that follows (Children will have art or music class at this time.).

Together with my letter I enclose some reading material, the results of useful staff development sessions I have attended. They have titles like "Helping Your Child Become a Lifelong Reader—Recommended Books," or "How to Select Books for Reading Aloud that You Too Can Enjoy." From the very beginning, I want parents to understand that we are undertaking a journey together, and they have specific roles to play. We will educate your child. The job will be easier, more fun, and more successful if the parent and the school work together.

As a teacher in an inner-city school, I am always aware of a characteristic that distinguishes some of our parents from those of affluent suburban communities. Over and over parents tell me that it is the job of the school to educate their child. Perhaps having spotty educations themselves, they lack confidence. However I know that the job that they do (readiness activities before kindergarten, family trips, daily checking of homework and book bag for notices, providing nutritious meals, seeing that children get adequate sleep, providing safe conduct to and from school, lots of love praise and support) is just as important as the job that I do.

3

Ten Sensational Books with which to Begin the Year

THE FIRST STORYTELLING SESSIONS of the year are very, very important. A major goal of the kindergarten teacher is to make the children love learning. It is true that we have to teach the class to read and write. However, this becomes extremely easy once they love stories and books and want to learn how to read and write. Parents have frequently told me how their young children nag and bedevil them when they really want to learn. When they see the others actually writing their own stories and standing up and reading to their classmates, children often begin a sustained campaign, complaining, whining, and demanding that their parents teach them too. How do I know this? The parents then come to me expressing helplessness. "He's driving me crazy," they say . . . then "What should I do?" While I tutor them so that they learn the necessary techniques to supplement my program, I continue to emphasize the importance of reading to their children daily, of reading colorful, enchanting picture books with exciting narratives within them. I've included some of my favorites here. Many of these are considered classics because they have satisfied generations of children. How do I, as a teacher, identify a classic?

1. A classic is a book that never goes out of print.
2. I truly never tire of reading a classic to the children.
3. These beloved books appeal to children of many ages. Little kids love them, but their big brothers and sisters will sit and listen contentedly also.
4. Classics have enduring messages or themes encompassing important values (i.e., courage, persistence, love, being adventurous, having good character traits, not antisocial ones).
5. Many favorite classics have plotlines with much repetition so that young children can chime in, actually memorizing them.
6. Frequently these stories illuminate other cultures so that children learn that people around the world are very much alike.

These are my surefire hits for the first month of school:

☆ *The Three Billy Goats Gruff,* S. Carpenter. HarperCollins, 1998. This is a well-known Nordic folk tale. Encourage the children to chime in. Say, "When you know the words, say them with me." Also use this story when you are teaching spatial relations (big, middle size, small) and phonics sounds, capital and lowercase.

☆ *The Puppy Who Went to School,* G. Herman. Grosset and Dunlap, 1959. This book is small, with charming illustrations. It is one of many stories about animals that come to school with a small child, who is experiencing this major transition (from home to school). Kindergarteners identify with the puppy who makes mistakes, who gets into trouble. It is a comforting story.

☆ *Whose Mouse Are You?* R. Kraus, Aladdin. 1970. When I read this story, the children like it so much, they immediately want to hear it again. So first, read it for fun. Then read it before a discussion of family ties and responsibilities. This story suggests the power that a youngster has in maintaining loving relationships.

☆ *Love You Forever*, R. Munsch. Firefly Books, 2000. There can never be too many stories about loving. This story celebrates the parent-child bond. I dare you to read it without getting a lump in your throat. The children are always deeply touched.

☆ *Madeline*, L. Bemelmans. Viking, 2000. Another classic that can be read over and over. Valuable as a tool for emphasizing auditory discrimination using rhyming but also positive in presenting a daredevil character who delights. This story introduces another cultural environment (France) that can be related to current events and television and also the language experiences of Caribbean and African classmates where French is spoken in the home.

☆ *Jamaica's Find*, J. Havill. Houghton Mifflin, 1986. A lovely, simple story that children can identify with. Jamaica looks like half the little girls in my class. This story stresses the development of morality and the growth of character.

☆ *Dora*. P. Beinstein. Simon and Schuster, 2003. This is one of the popular Dora the Explorer series. This is a charming book with colorful, big pictures. It is sturdily constructed. Dora introduces her friends and describes their activities. Each sentence in English is accompanied by a translation in Spanish. This book would be very comforting to a child who is not yet fluent in English.

☆ *The Snowy Day*, E. J. Keats. Viking, 1962. Visually stunning book with a simple story of an African American boy and his day in the snow. Always a great "read" after the first snowfall. A must for every kindergarten library.

☆ *Corduroy*, D. Freeman. Viking, 1968. Another appealing story that small children can relate to. Here a teddy bear gets lost in a department store. The bear's owner is a female of color.

☆ *Mufaro's Beautiful Daughters*, J. Steptoe. Lothrop, Lee and Shepard, 1987. One of the most enchanting books available. The illustrations are extraordinary. Set in Africa, this is a variation on the Cinderella tale. Because the language gets a little murky, it is better for the teacher to read the story to understand the plot, then tell the story to the class. This is the kind of book that stirs the imagination and sharpens the awareness of what is beautiful. John Steptoe dedicated this book to the children of South Africa.

4

The Second Day—Language Arts

ON THE SECOND DAY of school, after our "welcome song" and a finger play, we begin "readiness activities." While the children sit on the rug, we begin to attune their ears to the phonic "deluge" that is coming. By this I mean that the entire year's curriculum revolves around the children's solid knowledge of phonics. They must know the sound or variation in sounds *of each alphabet letter*, they must recognize them in combinations (i.e., blends), and use them to figure out new words. After all, letter "b" and "d" are not so different and letter "a" as in apple and letter "e" as in eggs probably sound alike to a young child. They must learn to hear subtle differences among sounds if they are to understand and use them correctly. So we begin auditory discrimination training with a game. Our first task is to focus on sounds, then to hear differences. This training goes hand and glove with finger plays, nursery rhymes, clapping games and jump-rope patters. I start with big distinctions.

LISTENING GAMES

The children turn away from me and hide their faces. Most of them sprawl on the rug and laugh with pleasure. When they are quiet and not peeking, I ring a little bell. They all scream, "It's a bell." Next, I clap my hands. Then I sneeze. Next I am asking them to hide their eyes, listen for the sound, then raise their hands so that I can call on someone. Next I tear a piece of paper, then use shears to making a cutting sound. The sounds are getting more subtle but the class is fully engaged. For the next week I will take time each day to play the auditory discrimination game so that they begin to listen carefully. Eventually I will give them first four, then three words, and they must clap when they hear a word that has a different beginning sound.

For example:

☆ Book ball berry song (First they listen, then teacher repeats and then they clap.)
☆ Rug rose kettle ring (Exaggerate initial sounds a lot!)
☆ Doughnut doctor lamp
☆ Water zebra window

After perhaps fifteen minutes of auditory games, it is time for a couple of songs, some finger plays and possibly a circle game like "Hokeypokey." You know . . .

You put your right foot in, you put your right foot out,
You put your right foot in, and you shake it all about,
You do the Hokey Pokey and you turn yourself around,
That's what it's all about. (Kids yell *"Hokey pokey!"*)

Continue . . . put the left foot in, the right and left hand, the head in, finally "your whole self" in.

TRIP AROUND THE SCHOOL

After toileting, on the second day, I like to take the class on a trip around the school. They need to feel comfortable in this new environment and get a sense where things are. They are being exposed to new people, hundreds of new children, and may feel adrift in a huge building with countless stairways and doors. Before we leave, I explain my expectations. They must hold a partner's hand. In the classrooms, children are working, so they may not talk in the hallways; however, they may whisper on the staircase (herein a discussion of whispering and how it differs from talking). I always end these sessions with the comment, "I want to be proud of you."

I like to begin in the office. Because they are very quiet, they are allowed to come in. I hope that I can lure the principal out. Principals are delighted by these situations because they see important socialization going on. The "kindergarten babies" are learning about their environment and the significant people in it. The principal is being introduced as someone to respect, someone who will have an important impact on their lives. In our building, the principal (always a woman) greets them, indeed charms them, but lets them know that her opinion of them is important. If the climate is right, I always ask them to recite "The Little Turtle" for her. (See, this kind of performance is the first of many, leading to a class of children who are comfortable in speaking, reciting, and also thinking on their feet.) When the principal returns to her office, I introduce the secretary and office personnel. Because I am always sending monitors to the office with attendance folders, notes and requests, it is valuable for them to know where to put things and who can help them. (Always send two children, with a pass and it never hurts to remind them not to run in the hallway.)

If these areas are empty, we might visit the gym and the auditorium. If the nurse is not busy she will say "hello" because she always has a message for them (i.e., "Don't forget to give Mommy messages from the nurse right away." "Don't run in the hallway or up the stairs.")

Our First Experience Chart (For Group Reading)

On our return to the classroom, we immediately do an experience chart. I take lined chart paper and ask the class what we saw. As the children respond, I write their names, a hyphen, and then their comments. (The principal said "Hello.") On the first day, there will not be an overwhelming response but in time we can easily fill up two pages. We will take the time to read the chart together. I will let the respondents read their lines because they take such pride in seeing their names and their words. However in succeeding days anybody can read them. The reader merely points to the child's name and intones, "Sarah says the teacher was angry because the class was talking on the stairs." If the grammar is correct, I write it as they say it. This material is quickly memorized by the children and they take pleasure in "reading" to each other, pointer in hand. The significance is that they are seeing "heavy-duty" words like, "the," "was," "class," "on," which they remember and as their phonic skills kick in, they really begin to read. Teaching reading is really quite easy!

Children learn a repertoire of "sight" words like "the," which cannot be sounded out phonetically, at the same time that they use phonics to figure out words that they do not know. Constant exposure to print in the form of labels, book titles, chart stories, sentences that they copy, homework practice, "easy readers," signs, newspaper titles and by Thanksgiving the great adventure has begun for most of them. If that sounds too grandiose, all I can say is that reading is the joy of my life and if I do my job right this year, it will also be theirs.

In the days that follow, routines are quickly established. Young children relax into routines. They enjoy predictable events. Since they are learning a whole new set of skills, they need the security of what is known, of what they did before. So do I. Because my body clock is nocturnal I stagger into the classroom, semi-awake. The quiet talking time on the rug (which quickly becomes a quiet reading time) gives me the time to examine notices, set up my charts, chat informally with children and generally recover from the trauma of the subway. By the time full-day sessions have begun, the morning looks like this:

DAILY SCHEDULE

8:30–9:00 A.M.	Clothing away, homework or home notices collected, picture books chosen and taken to the rug. Talking is discouraged.

9:00–10:00–A.M.

WELCOME SONG:	"We Are Glad To See You" or "Good Morning to You."
ATTENDANCE:	Each child responding, "I am here" using a sentence. *Several finger plays.*
A MORNING MESSAGE:	This can be anything—"I like school" or, "Our Trip around P.S. 207," read aloud.
BIG BOOK LESSON (MONDAY, TUESDAY, THURSDAY):	One book chosen for the week with one new "teaching point" daily. Teacher can help class to see beginning sounds that are similar, "sight words" that they know.
CRITICAL THINKING LESSON (WEDNESDAY):	Write children's comments on chart.
WEEKLY READER LESSON (FRIDAY):	Page four is discussed as a group, but children are instructed to return to seats and finish on their own. Correct papers get a red check; incorrect papers are reviewed with the child. In September and October, the paper is read by the teacher. Children are encouraged to speculate and read words that they know. By February and March enough children can read the *Weekly Reader* so that teacher focuses on inferences and interpretation.

10:00–10:20 A.M.

TOILETING:　　　　　　　The whole class goes out.

10:20–10:50 A.M.　　　　Mathematics.

10:50–11:40 A.M.

LUNCH:　　　　　　　　With outdoor play.

11:40–12:10 P.M.

REST TIME:　　　　　　Most children will sleep at their desks but the non-sleepers might read quietly.

12:10–12:40 P.M.　　　　Story time.

12:40–1:30 P.M.

PREP PERIODS:　　　　　(I am blocking *Prep Periods* into this space, however, they may be scheduled at any time, morning or afternoon. When making up your weekly schedule, block in *Prep Periods* first, such as music, health education, art.)

1:30–2:10 P.M.

SCIENCE:　　　　　　　(Monday, Wednesday, Friday)

SOCIAL STUDIES:　　　　(Tuesday, Thursday)

2:10–2:45 P.M.　　　　　Choice time.

2:45–3:00 P.M.

CLEANUP:　　　　　　　Distribution of notices, clothing, dismissal.

Remember, nothing is written in stone. You may begin your lesson and someone walks in and says there is a fire drill in ten minutes. While conducting a book talk or a story time, someone may walk in and tell you that they are here to give you a prep period to make up for one that you did not get. Visitors constantly appear with the principal. Just remember that you must take the time to train the children to take visitors in stride. They must continue with the lesson, may not run over and engage the visitor. I usually tell them that people come to see what they are learning so they must sit quietly if someone enters the classroom. Sometimes I let them recite a poem or let them read an experience chart for guests. It is very effective if a child becomes the teacher and leads them. It is also a good idea to train several children to function like tour guides when visitors appear. They can be trained to walk the visitors around the room explaining charts, displays, and class projects. This is such an effective tool in developing social skills and cementing knowledge (you know, the easiest way to cement knowledge is to teach someone else). I honestly think the whole class could take turns doing this job.

During the first month, repetition is very important. Routines must be internalized (so that children know exactly what to do).

Everyday Routines

Attendance—Line the children up—boys on one side, girls on the other. The class counts girls, boys, then the total. On the first day of school, I can always find a volunteer to write the numbers (although I might have to demonstrate first.) For daily attendance you need to laminate a chart with a boy figure, a girl figure, and then two figures together. Let your mathematical helper record the numbers with a dry marking pen so that the numbers can be erased with a tissue daily. This is an easy way for them to learn to count, to add, to get an understanding of gender and to line up.

COLOR CHARTS—LEARNING COLORS

To tell the truth, I do the same things year after year. I carry my curriculum around in my head. In fact, I write my lesson plans after the lesson (usually during lunch). But that's all right because, barring some tantalizing new strategy, there's a rhythm to the activities of a year and the same things fall in place at appropriate times. For example, as I notice the leaves on the trees in the small playground turn bright red, it is time to cut out oaktag the size of a greeting card and using a black marker draw part of a limb and part of a trunk. The children color the trunk and limb. Then the whole class goes outside to gather the small intensely red leaves, which we paste onto the tree. It is fun to bunch the leaves together in a natural way so they appear to be hanging from the tree. With black Magic Markers the children write something as simple as "I like fall." By this time they all know the words "fall" and "like" from the morning message so they can take the card home and read it to their parents.

I usually do color charts the first week of school. As a homework assignment I ask the children to cut out something red from a magazine. Here I am no more than reinforcing prekindergarten work. It is rare these days for children to enter kindergarten without knowing their colors. So I am not teaching colors. Instead I am finding out if they comprehend the concepts. When they return with their pictures we will glue them to a chart and label the objects. Several things are important here. 1) We are understanding that objects have names, which we must learn. 2) Also we want to develop the homework habit. In some form, it is a nightly assignment. 3) We are learning to remember. In becoming independent beings, children must move away from parents, must less and less depend on them to remember for them. Homework assignments are the child's responsibility.

It is a good thing if they can begin to train themselves to do mental tasks. Since they cannot write yet, they can be responsible for remembering to do homework daily. Mothers often say, "Just write me a note in Mia's notebook." I prefer to see the child developing a sense of discipline about remembering. But do not be deceived. I make telephone calls, waylay parents in the morning, etc.

Name Tags

Only use for the first week, they are usually a mess after a while. Besides the teacher must learn names as quickly as possible. The name-tag game is played each morning. Names are printed on oak-tag and holes are punched at the ends. Knitting yarn is best for the string that goes around the child's neck.

THE CALENDAR

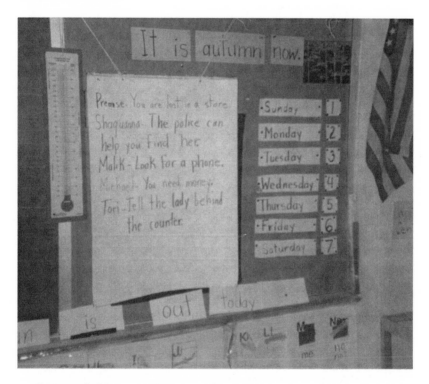

Giving children authentic information gives them power. By knowing, they gain control of their world. They want to know when Halloween is coming, how many days to their birthday . . . So teaching the calendar gives knowledge (more cultural capital). As we begin a new month and often during the week, I like to have the class say this poem:

THE CALENDAR SAYS SEPTEMBER

The calendar says September (or appropriate month)

The clock says nine a.m.

It's autumn and we're sitting (or appropriate season)

Back in school again

When we see our friends, we'll wave. (Pantomime waving)

When we're in school, we will behave.

We'll read from books and write our names

And play some of our favorite games.

DAYS OF THE WEEK

Sunday 1

Monday 2

Tuesday 3

Wednesday 4

Thursday 5

Friday 6

Saturday 7

SIMON SAYS (FOR PARTS OF THE BODY)

Simple Simon says put your hands on your: head, back, neck, elbows, thighs, ears, toes, wrist, calves, legs, stomach, knees, ankles, shoulders, biceps, nose, chin, chest, hips, eyebrows, etc.

Start easy but get more difficult over time. Wait while the children find each part. If they have difficulty, just show them. This exercise is perfect as a transition activity or when the class is getting out of control.

THE WEATHER

The weather can be discussed in the morning message. Also a circular chart with symbols and the words sunny, rainy, cloudy, snowy, is valuable in recording events in their lives. The teacher can make an arrow and attach it with a paper clip. Weather reports are also a means of acquiring vocabulary. Whenever there is a major snowstorm, we do an experience chart, describing the streets, our houses, problems we had in getting to school.

DAYS OF THE WEEK: I usually create a permanent chart with the days. Beside Sunday, I write the numeral one; after Monday the numeral two. In this way we learn time concepts but also ordinal numbers (See page 35). My associate Sherman Beattie made up a song for this material:

Today is Monday,

Today is Monday,

Today is Monday

The second day of the week.

Yesterday was Sunday,

Yesterday was Sunday,

Yesterday was Sunday,

The first day of the week.

Tomorrow will be Tuesday,

Tomorrow will be Tuesday,

Tomorrow will be Tuesday,

The third day of the week.

      —R. Sherman Beattie

DAILY READING ROUTINES—THE MORNING MESSAGE—BACKSTORY . . .

A few years back we were introduced, yet again, to a new reading system. New teachers, you will find that approximately every four years, we are exposed to a new reading program. Recently, we were introduced to *Bookshop: A Balanced Literacy Program*, also known as MONDO. (Greenvale, N.Y., Mondo Publishing, 1995, 1998)

The annoying thing about this quadriannual torture is that at some point after a few years of staff development, you have learned the new system, but the workshops continue, old methods that work are ignored and you must adhere to the new instructional materials. Ultimately you do not get a chance to do what works. For example, when I reentered the school system in 1984, I had become convinced that phonics was the best way to teach disadvantaged children to read. They would learn the sound of each letter and by combining sounds they could puzzle out words. While I was teaching at Rutgers University, Lucy Caulkins at Teachers College had started the "whole language" approach and phonics was less emphasized as a necessary ingredient in achieving reading success.

Every teacher was forced to go to workshops and more workshops where the new method was taught. An old pro like me eventually becomes subversive and gives them a little of what they want (you have to bring copies of the children's work to the workshops). Meanwhile, I close my classroom door and do what I like. I justify this in several ways. First of all, I really do know how to teach reading. After thirty-one years with the Department of Education, I would have to be a dolt not to know. At the end of the day, my success rates tell me that I have done the right thing. In the 1960s two educators, Postman and Weingartner, wrote a book called, *Teaching as a Subversive Activity* (1969). I have adopted this view because administrators seem frequently not to be educators. When I began teaching in my fourth school, I learned that my new principal had been a gym teacher. I had become contemptuous of gym teachers as I watched our staff person sitting outside in the yard, drinking coffee, and reading the newspapers as the kids ran screaming around the yard. I must say that a gym instructor at Teachers College, Columbia University changed my thinking as I saw a superlative instructional period where solid conceptual learning took place during gym. (A wag once told me that many gym teachers become principals because they are more able to hide from administrators and study for the license exams.) Nevertheless one becomes subversive because the "best practices" that one has learned are ignored as the next new reading system is hammered into place. And while the desire, to have uniform instruction going on in every classroom, so that there is some standardization in what all children are learning, (standardization is the mantra of this generation of chancellors and section heads), let's all remember that really talented teachers are rarely "team players" and really great teachers are almost never "team players." Great teachers transcend institutions; they create environments that work for them. They drag faculties and administrators and students behind them. (I used to sit in sociological theorist Robert Merton's class at Columbia University. I did not go to Columbia. I am sure that a large number of the students sitting in his class didn't either. However talent is drawn to talent and young people are always looking for leaders to inspire them. If you were orderly in Merton's class, you could stay and learn.) Readers of this book are either new teachers or teachers who are willing to learn more about the pedagogy of early childhood. Step right this way . . .

THE MORNING MESSAGE (CONTINUED)

The Morning Message is a two- or three-line blurb that gets printed on a large lined pad daily. This is a teaching strategy that works in many classrooms (MONDO did not invent this device because experienced teachers have been writing something on the board since one-room schoolhouses were the norm). The idea is to settle the class down and get them working quickly. The message is something like:

"Today is Tuesday, November 12, 2011. It is a rainy day. Tomorrow we will have a party."

In most first grade classes the teacher would expect the students to copy the message in their notebooks. Then it is read, discussed, added to (a word or two might have to be decoded). In September, I like to begin my first message with the following sentence: "I like school." I do not ask them to write the words but I do an experience chart where I write their comments. We do lots of "I like . . ." charts. Prompts like, "What do you like to do on Saturday?" "What is your favorite food?" get them talking. Then I write the child's name—a dash—then the child's comment. I want them to learn the words, "I" and "like" because they are meaningful and fun. They are also "heavy-duty" words that the children will use a lot. Sometimes it is necessary to reword their comments. For example, if a child says, "Her takes me to the park." I say in a neutral, informational way, "In school we say, 'She takes me to the park.'" Children are usually so mesmerized at seeing their names in print that the correction does not sting. The experience charts (so numerous that we hang them on clotheslines around the room) will be read over and over daily. During Choice Time, children love to take a pointer and read these charts to their classmates. It is also helpful to clip them together into giant storybooks for reading with a friend or so children can glance at them when they are lining up or passing by. Young children are sponges, constantly taking in information.

Experience charts and Morning Messages are crucial parts of my language arts program. We use them after all major holidays. Children love to tell what happened while trick-or-treating, about their winter and spring holidays, birthday celebrations held in school. We use them to record favorite songs, to retell stories, to remember finger plays and jump-rope patters. In this way we build up a repertoire of "cultural capital," language patterns, correct grammar and usage and also correct spellings. What better way to learn poetry and parts of speeches? For years I would write down the last part of Dr. Martin Luther King's "I Have a Dream" speech.

The class would learn to read it, memorize it, and recite it as part of our January assembly.

Kindergarten children are amazing. They have not learned to feel inadequate about their abilities so they jump right in and learn. Because they are so fearless and curious about everything, I love to develop their thinking skills. It is a joy to present them with problems to ponder. It is a perfect time to train them to look at problems and suggest possible solutions. As long as the teacher is not judgmental or disapproving they love to generate scenarios, some wacky, some imaginative, some ingenious. The following are actual experience charts with the child's responses. During Playtime or Discovery Time, one activity is for two or three children to use a pointer and read the experience charts, which may be hanging on the walls or hanging on clotheslines stretched overhead. Of course, at first, they are merely "parroting" what they remember. But the "heavy-duty" words (i.e., I, go, talk) become familiar and together with their own names and words that have emotional resonance (i.e., Mommy, love, train) are remembered. Sylvia Ashton Warner understood and used these techniques in New Zealand with great success.

Accomplished teachers understand that "heavy-duty" words and emotionally powerful words, combined with increasing skill in phonics so that students can decode words that they don't know, make reading success possible. Once a word is learned and the child can recognize it anywhere . . . that's *reading*.

September Experience Charts (Here are some excellent sidebars. These were actually created by my kindergarteners.)

 OUR TRIP AROUND P.S. 207

NEIL: I saw the office. (*The repeated use of the words *I, saw, was, the, we* is very important. These are words that must be memorized quickly. They are "heavy-duty.")

RANDY: I saw the nurse.

CARY: I saw the stage.

TYRONE: I saw seats.

JASMINE: I was at the principal's office.

SAQUAN: We went to the library.

AMINAH: I saw the stairs.

ALEXIS: I saw the piano.

SARA: I saw the playground.

TROY: We walked downstairs.

 OUR TRIP TO THE 115TH STREET LIBRARY

Children are being nudged into using full sentences. The teacher starts them off by merely saying "I . . ." and then she waits. The child gets the message.

JARED: I saw Wadleigh Junior High School.

TRAVIS: We saw lots of churches.

JASMINE: I saw restaurants.

CHANTELL: The Africans and the Americans cook the food.

QYDELL: They gave us yellow sheets. If Mommy signs, we get library cards.

 (NOVEMBER) OUR TRIP TO THE AMERICAN MUSEUM OF NATURAL HISTORY

EBONY: We went on a school bus.

ALEX: We went to the planetarium.

VON MARIE: I saw Big Bird up in the sky.

JERRY: I learned about rainbows.

CORY: You see rainbows when the sun is behind you and water comes down.

TYRONE: I saw shooting stars.

LARRY: I counted stars.

SHIRELL: I counted 1, 2, 3, and the sky turned blue.

BRIAN: I saw Barosaurus.

BRYAN: I saw Tyrannosaurus Rex.

TYRELL: The dinosaur opened his mouth.

LUZ: We saw dinosaur eggs.

CANDACE: The bones and eggs turned to stone.
QYDELL: They are fossils now.

From these charts it is clear that my kindergarteners were learning many things. They increasingly spoke in sentences. They were developing knowledge about their school, their neighborhood, about science. They have been storing up what is clearly "cultural capital." This is information that they absorb as they move through the grades. For example, what they learn about dinosaurs in kindergarten can be built on in high school and then in college as the study of *paleontology*. The visit to the planetarium introduces them to *astronomy*. As their reading skills grow, and their interests develop they can create lifelong passions or long-term careers. Most importantly, children learn to analyze events or experiences and see relationships between events, ideas, and elements. Because we want children to be able to think and behave effectively, the ability to analyze has critical value in their educational experience (Bloom, B. S., 1956). The following examples show the children's intellectual growth as they are presented with new environments, interesting problems, and verbal challenges during the school year.

 PROBLEM: COMPARE A SUNFLOWER AND A GLOBE
(USED IN TEACHING GEOGRAPHY).

What is different?

MORGAN: The sunflower has a stem. The globe doesn't.
GREGORY: The globe is hard. The sunflower is soft.
ELIJAH: The sunflower drinks water and grows. The globe doesn't drink. It doesn't grow either.
JESSICA: The globe has lines on it. The sunflower doesn't.
RASHEIN: The sunflower needs sun. The globe doesn't need sun.

What is similar?

SUSIE: They both are round.

NAQUAN: The globe spins around. The sunflower turns around to the sun.

PEARL: The globe has colors. The sunflower has colors.

KEYANA: They both have stems.

BYRIN: They both have yellow colors.

Compare a snail and a cat. What is the same?

LORRIE: They both eat food.

BYRON: They both have eyes.

SEAN: They both move.

HASEEM: They both have soft bodies.

WILLIE: They both have mouths.

MARIA: They both have heads.

What is different?

TYRONE: A cat has a tail. The snail doesn't.

ROSA: The cat has legs. The snail doesn't.

LON: The cat has hair. The snail doesn't.

KEYANA: The cat has teeth. The snail doesn't.

JENAY: The snail has tentacles. The cat doesn't.

JOSE: The snail has a slimy trail. The cat doesn't.

WHY OUR SCHOOL WAS FAILING!

P.S. 207 was in a low income area. When I was able to locate a printout of the citywide reading scores, I looked for my school to see how we performed in relation to other schools. I thought I was reading a misprint. The statistics showed that fourteen percent of my school's students were reading on grade level. Good grief! That meant that eighty-six percent of them were not. Add to this the fact that the turnover in faculty was appalling. A parade of young teachers would come and go, relocate to suburban schools, or get married, and apparently need to join their spouses in other cities. If they were new teachers and lacked strong classroom management skills and had yet to internalize the elements of a curriculum (meaning that when you walked into the class in September, you already had the year's curriculum in your head and you knew exactly what you would be doing in March), they were in for a rocky ride. Most of the children were manageable but a large number were out of control. The level of aggression, the fist fights, the cursing, the enraged children who would knock over chairs, throw things at the teacher and, indeed, hit the teacher, had to be frightening to young people who had gone to stable middle-class schools. Getting married and moving on was one way of getting out; taking tests and becoming guidance counselors or administrators or staff developers was another. I had already logged sixteen years in elementary school and a substantial number in college teaching, and it was clear to me that a school could sustain a few new teachers from time to time, but the wholesale flight of teachers meant a revolving staff of beginners who would not get the stable climate in which to develop the craft and the art of teaching. We had low reading scores. We had new teachers who left before they had skills, and we had a large number of out-of-control kids. We were in big trouble.

5

Beginning Reading . . . and Writing

THE ALPHABET

OBVIOUSLY, BEGINNING TO READ involves the alphabet. In my Harlem kindergarten class we begin reading activities the second week of an all-day program. I had begun to realize that practically every child comes to kindergarten knowing the alphabet song ("*A, B, C, D, E, F*, G . . ." to the tune of "Twinkle, Twinkle, Little Star"). It all derives from preschool graduations, where, across the nation, pre-Ks usually sing the song to their delighted parents in June. The letters and their sequence have been firmly planted in their minds, although they don't generally know what the letters signify. My literacy program is grounded in "phonics," using those very letters. My approach to reading is quite different from most educators . . . but it is highly successful. An important piece is that I stress phonics, phonics, and more phonics. Back in the 1980s when the "whole language" method was the "next big thing" in education, phonics was not stressed. American educators misunderstood the reading styles of the New Zealand and Australian "infant schools" who did not stress phonics but who did include it as an ingredient in their teaching method. When told to ignore phonics, I went into my class-room and closed the door and taught phonics anyway. After thirty years in early childhood education, I trust my own judgment.

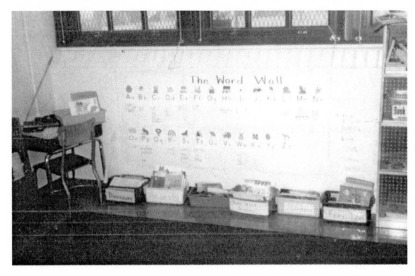

What is "phonics" all about? Each letter of the alphabet has a characteristic sound. Some of them have more than one. Another way of saying this, in more technical terms, is to say that *pho-nics* describes an area of knowledge that includes the most com-mon sounds of the English language and the letters that represent these sounds. For example, letter *a* has the long sound of *ate* and the short sound of *apple*. Some letters share sounds (letter *k* in *kite* and letter *c* as in *cat*). Each child must learn these sounds as well as the *hard* and *soft* sounds (*g* as in *go* and *g* as in *engine*).

★ SAMPLE LESSON: LEARNING PHONIC SOUNDS

Place on the table an assortment of letters:

t, a, b, s, s, m, m,

Slide s out from the bunch.

SAY   This is s̲. (Teacher says the sound.) Say it with me!

Child repeats the sound.

Place child's finger on the flocked (or sandpaper) letter.

SAY   Trace the s̲. It looks like a . . . snake.

SAY   Say s̲. Mix all the letters up (but keep s̲ separate).

SAY   Find me one like s̲.

        Child finds an s̲. (If child slides the letter upside down—point to the original.)

SAY   Make it look like this one.

SAY   What is this sound? (Child repeats.)

SAY   What begins with s̲?

        Give answers if child doesn't respond (i.e. snake, sun, singing, sky). Have child repeat these.

SAY   This is m̲. (Teacher says sound.) Say it with me! Child repeats.

        Place child's finger on flocked (or sandpaper) letter.

SAY   Trace the m̲.

SAY   Say m̲.

        Mix all the letters up (keeping m separate).

SAY   Find me one like this m̲.

SAY   Make it look like this one.

SAY   What is this sound?

        Child repeats.

SAY   What begins with m̲? (Prompt if no response.) Mommy, monkey, moon, money, milk.

This game may be played continuously until the child knows his/her phonic sounds. If flocked or sandpaper letters are not available the teacher may cut out oaktag letters, But the tactile tracing together with the verbal responses and visual identification really helps to fix the sounds in the child's memory.

How to begin? On the first day of school, parents received a notice requesting that they purchase two composition books for their child. These are to be brought to school as quickly as possible. We label them and stack them where a child monitor can retrieve them and return them. In a perfect world, the school would purchase primary paper, with lines that indicate where capitals begin and a dotted line that shows where lower case letters are written. However, my school never had primary paper.

I used the money allocated by the department for basic supplies. So I became reconciled to black-and-white composition books, bought by my parents, because they represented an investment that a parent has made in the child's reading experience. Believe me, during parent conferences, those books are examined carefully by Mom and Dad.

I always begin the alphabet with letter *a*. Experts suggest that we should begin with a letter like *m* because the sound is easier to remember. I have observed that we teach them the alphabet song . . . with the correct sequence . . . and then begin with letter *m*. That's too complicated. Let's start with *Aa*.

Composition books and pencils are given out. Some little mischief makers will manage to break their pencil points, so have a supply. Children must turn to the first page. The teacher will show them how to fold the paper in half so there are two sides. The teacher will then whip out a large piece of newsprint paper and attach it to a surface. Sometimes I have a writing stand, but an easel or paper attached to a bulletin board will do. She (or he) will use a black crayon and draw seven evenly spaced lines across the paper with a line down the middle. Each time we learn a letter, I let the class watch me draw the lines because I believe they get a sense of the task (they are focusing on the lines, the placement of the letters, the spatial relations involved). They are internalizing the way writing paper looks and where letters are placed. This is one of those moments where they all watch me and are mesmerized by the ritual. The teacher makes a capital *A* on one side of the paper and a lower case *a* on the other side. The children seem hypnotized. This is serious stuff. The capitals go on the left, the lowercases on the right.

Teacher: Children, this is the letter *A*. Say the letter with me . . . A . . . Here is capital A . . . and here is lowercase *a*. The sound of *a* is *a*. (*Apple*) Can you think of something else that begins with *a*? (If you don't get a response help them out with . . .

alligator, ambulance, aunt.) You can say, "What does Mommy call when someone has to go to the hospital? What is the sound again? Now let's write it in the air."

I verbalize the writing like this . . . For capital *A* . . . I also write in the air with them and say:

"Slant down . . . slant down . . . across . . . Let's do it again . . ." The class will write capital *A* in the air three times. Then they pick up their pencils while I tell them that capital *A* takes up two spaces. I touch the page . . . one space . . . two spaces . . . Capitals are big letters . . . What is the sound of *A*? Let's write . . . Slant down . . . slant down . . . across . . .

For lower case *a* I say, "Let's write it in the air . . . circle and down . . . Let's do it again . . ."

Circle and down . . . (Three times) What's the sound? Then I say, "Pick up your pencils . . . Remember that lowercase *a* only takes up one space . . .

Write . . . Circle and down . . . Make it round like a ball . . . and the down stroke begins up high on the side . . ."

Teacher tips . . .

Only focus on one thing at a time. Do not mention long *a* (*ate*). Save that for a later time. Two much information at one time is confusing. Since the children are lying or sitting on the rug as they write, you can actually see their books and what they are doing. Don't hesitate to ask a child to hold up their book if you can't see their work. I like to hold up correct work so that everybody can see it. Be lavish with your praise. "Kahlil, that's sensational. Show the class." Contrary to most kindergartens, we learn letters in two sessions weekly. While I know teachers who pride themselves on completing the whole alphabet in the first two weeks of the year, in my class we take it very slowly. We give students ample time to assimilate this new knowledge. As new letters are learned, they are incorporated and discussed during Morning Meeting, the daily message that we review, in homework and into experience charts.

One additional comment . . . as students write at least three images of the alphabet letter, if the work is well executed, make a big red check across the page. Where the child has had difficulty, turn to the back of the page and write the letters at the top and suggest that they do it again.

Since this is the day's homework, try to solve as many problems in class as possible. Where the work is messy and sloppy, I give a small check at the top, for "prodigious effort." I want the child to know it could be better but "it's getting there." In every case, it is important for the child to understand that there are standards that they should meet.

Even if I accept less than perfect work now (and I often do with a first effort), I am always nudging them, with gentleness and humor, toward excellence. Remember that the homework assignment is practice of that day's alphabet letter.

Review the last letter taught by holding up the capital and lowercase letter ($A \ldots a$).

"Now we fold our paper in two . . ." The teacher writes on chart paper . . . B . . . Next . . . we say . . . "Children . . . this is letter B . . . Say the letter with me . . . B . . ." (Teacher writes):

"Here is capital B and here is lowercase b. The sound of B is (*bat*). Say it with me. . . B . . . Let's say it again . . . B . . . Can you think of something in this classroom that begins with this sound?" They may be able to say . . . *book* . . . *boy* . . . *bell* . . . *bottle*. At the top of the page I might write *Bat*." I will remind them of letter a and its sound and include t but do not dwell on it.

"What is our new sound?" Point to B. "Let's write it in the air . . ."

I verbalize the writing like this . . . "For capital B. . . (I write with them) . . . it is . . . down . . . around . . . in . . . then out . . . around . . . and . . . in again. Let's do that again (three times) . . ." Then they pick up their pencils, and I remind them that capital B will take up two spaces . . . and we form the letter.

"Down . . . around . . . in . . . then out . . . around . . . and in again . . . What is the sound of letter B?

"Now we are ready to do the lowercase *b* . . . It is a lowercase letter, but it is also two spaces high . . . In the air let's write . . . down and around . . . do it again . . . down and around (three times).

"Now let's write it on our paper . . . Down and around . . . Notice that the "around" part looks like a ball and it takes up a whole space. What's the sound?"

Tip . . .

The class will do three capitals and three lowercase letters in one lesson. For homework I would hand out a Xerox sheet. On each sheet I have written the capital and the lowercase letter at the top with a Magic Marker (red or blue) then I draw a line or a dot where the child is to form the letter. I don't want them to focus on lines or spacing. The task is simple . . . form the letter correctly. I usually make them do ten letters (five capital letters . . . five lowercase letters).

The next letter to be learned is capital *C* and lowercase *c*. The routine is the same for each letter.

"This is letter . . . Say the letter with me . . . Here is capital . . . and here is lowercase . . . The sound of . . . is . . . Can you think of something that begins with this sound? . . ." (Prompt . . .)

"What does Mommy reach for . . . What is the sound again? Now let's write it in the air . . . (three times)."

The following are my verbal prompts for each letter as we write (use a little rhythm).

- Capital *C* . . . Around and around and up.
- Lowercase *c* . . . Around and around and up.
- Capital *D* . . . Down stroke . . . Back to the top and around.
- Lowercase *d* . . . It's two spaces high . . . circle at the bottom . . . then down.
- Capital *E* . . . Down . . . out . . . out . . . out. See. It has three strokes . . . out . . . out . . . out.

- Lowercase *e* . . . Start in the middle of the space . . . straight out . . . around . . . around and up.
- Capital *F*. . . Down stroke . . . straight out . . . straight out . . . Notice . . . only two straight lines . . .
- Lowercase *f*. . . It's two spaces high . . . Start below the line . . . Go around and down . . . then cross . . .
- Capital *G*. . . It's almost a circle . . . Go around and around and around and in...
- Lowercase *g*. . . Don't start where the capital starts . . . go to the lower space . . . make a circle . . . then go down and around in a hook . . .
- Capital *H* . . . Down stroke . . . down stroke . . . across . . .
- Lowercase *h* . . . It's two spaces high . . . down . . . back up and around . . .
- Capital *I* . . . Down stroke . . . Put a hat on it . . . and shoes . . .
- Lowercase *i* . . . Don't start where the capital starts . . . start below . . . then down stroke . . . only one space . . . and put a dot . . .
- Capital *J* . . . Down . . . down . . . around and up.
- Lowercase *j* . . . Don't start where the capital starts . . . go to the lower space . . . Straight down . . . under the line . . . then make a hook . . .
- Capital *K* . . . Down stroke . . . Slant in . . . slant out . . .
- Lowercase *k* . . . Almost the same as the capital . . . Down stroke . . . but begin the slant in on the lower space.
- Capital *L* . . . Down stroke . . . straight out . . .
- Lowercase *l* . . . Down stroke . . . two spaces high . . .
- Capital *M* . . . Down stroke . . . slant in . . . this way . . . slant in . . . that way . . . and down.
- Lowercase *m* . . . This letter is one space high. . . Down stroke . . . up and around . . . up and around...and down.
- Capital *N* . . . Down stroke . . . slant . . . down stroke.
- Lowercase *n* . . . One space high . . . down stroke . . . up and around . . . and down.
- Capital *O* . . . Let's make a nice fat circle . . . around and around and around.

- Lowercase *o* . . . around and around and around.
- Capital *P* . . . Down stroke . . . back to the top . . . and around . . .
- Lowercase *p* . . . Begin in the lower space . . . Down stroke . . . go underneath the line . . . back to the top . . . and around.
- Capital *Q* . . . Make a circle . . . around and around and around . . . then make a tail.
- Lowercase *q* . . . Go to the lower space . . . make a circle . . . one space high . . . on the right side . . . go straight down under the line...add a little flag.
- Capital *R* . . . Down stroke . . . back to the top . . . around . . . down . . . go in . . . out on a slant.
- Lowercase *r* . . . Begin in the lower space . . . one space high . . . down . . . back up and over.
- Capital *S* . . . It looks like a snake . . . Start under the line . . . and go around and down and around . . . and up.
- Lowercase *s* . . . Begin in the lower space . . . around and down and around and up. It looks just like the capital.
- Capital *T* . . . Down stroke . . . two spaces . . . put a hat on it.
- Lowercase *t* . . . Two spaces high . . . down stroke . . . cross it in the middle.
- Capital *U* . . . Down and around and up.
- Lowercase *u* . . . Go to the lower space . . . down and around and up . . . and down.
- Capital *V* . . . Slant down . . . slant up . . .
- Lowercase *v* . . . On the lower space . . . slant down . . . slant up.
- Capital *W* . . . Slant down and up . . . and down . . . and up.
- Lowercase *w* . . . On the lower space... slant down and up and down and up...
- Capital *X* . . . Slant down . . . back to the top . . . slant and cross.
- Lowercase *x* . . . Go to the lower space . . . slant down . . . slant across.
- Capital *Y* . . . In the top space . . . make a *v* . . . then add a tail.
- Lowercase *y* . . . Start in the lower space . . . slant down . . . go under the line.

- Capital *Z* . . . *Across . . . then slant two spaces . . . go across again . . .*
- Lowercase *z* . . . Go to the lower space . . . across . . . slant down . . . and back again.

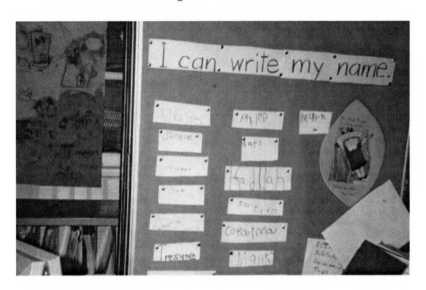

✎ OUR FIRST LITERARY TASK

"How to Write Your Name"

1. Have children write words that they see around the room.
2. Encourage them to write their names on work done in class. Check—there will be lots of capital letters.
3. Bean Pictures—to see how individual letters are written. Stress that we must learn to use capital and lowercase letters.
4. Name cards posted on tables. Stress that this is the way we write our names in school. Upper and lowercase letters used.
5. For homework, send a sheet with upper- and lowercase letters. (Daily practice.)
6. Practice: during writing periods give the children long strips of paper. Let them copy the name cards on their desks.

7. Practice: teacher gives out strips with a line drawn. Children must write on the line.

8. Create a chart to hang up. Title is "I can write my name." If a child can write his/her name in capitals and lowercase, post the card itself on the chart. If the work is totally illegible, they have to do it over. If it is clearly impossible, discontinue the task for a while (a few days) then have the child work one-on-one with the educational assistant.

9. Applause and recognition whenever a name is added to the chart.

THE FIRST BIG LITERARY TASK—WRITING OUR NAMES

The teacher begins with *Writing Our Names* in self-defense. Because we must be aware of the developmental progress that each child is making, we must have *portfolios* ready very quickly. All the child's work will be labeled daily and saved in individual portfolios or sent home to parents. Labeling each child's work takes up so much time that the sane and sensible thing is for *them* to do the job. Any kind of portfolio will do but I invest in plastic or cardboard magazine filers. I tape each child's name on and then stuff them with the day's work.

We begin the writing of names with *informal* exercises. Within the first week of school, I pass out drawing paper and crayons. I ask the children to write down any words that they see around the room. I tell them that this is a "practice" so they should do the best that they can. After fifteen minutes, I collect all the papers and give out a new sheet and encourage them to draw whatever they like. The first sheet is to get them to focus on the letters all around them, also to give me an idea of the skill level of each child. The second sheet is to relax those that are tense because they have had difficulty shaping letters. But make no mistake. After all writing lessons, I will continually ask the children to write their names on their papers. I want them to understand that "name-writing" will be expected of them but where they do not have the skill yet, I or my assistant will help them. This is a "shaping" situation where I am leading them toward a goal (writing names).

During this period, I expect to see lots of writing with capitals because this is what parents have been teaching them. I am grateful for the exertions of parents or caregivers, because a child who can write his name using capitals is focusing on the task and is already showing skills, so it is relatively easy for such a child to begin writing lowercase letters. What I am suggesting is that while the child must un-learn writing *all* capitals, that process is relatively easy at this stage. Teacher approval is important so a child can move to the next stage because the teacher is encouraging.

We begin the more *formal* phase by distributing strips of paper, about seven inches long and two inches wide. I point to the name taped to one child's desk. I ask, "What does this say?" The child may or may not recognize his or her own name but after I have walked around the room and asked the question of several students and ascertained that these are their names, I then ask, "Sara, where else is your name in this room?" One or two children are sent to point to their names on hooks in the coat closet, on the attendance chart, experience charts, on the homework chart. Before I ask them to write their name, using the letters that they see, we take a moment to count the letters. ("Kelvin, how many letters in your name?") It is worthwhile noting that Elizabeth has nine letters but Keli only has four letters. Then we begin writing. The children are highly motivated to learn this task because it is so personal. By the way, where children can write their name in capitals, we praise them mightily and show their classmates but at the same time we gently let them know that in school we write a different way. In school we use big and little letters. I let them know that I call them *capital* and *lowercase* letters. Name—writing can be a daily activity and a homework activity; however *I make a point of sending home a sheet for parents with upper- and lowercase letters written correctly. It is important for parents to see what the standards for this unit are.*

Bean Pictures

Most kindergartners enjoy the next step. To help them shape the letters we have a fun session shaping each letter with beans. The teacher gives each child a paper with his or her name printed on a line. I like to use the packages of black beans used by Cubans in making black bean soup. The printing must be sufficiently large so the children will have plenty of room to connect the beans as they shape each letter. They must try not to squeeze the letters together. During this period, the teacher and educational assistant are moving around the room encouraging and suggesting. At the same time our student is absorbing the shape of his name, which letters go above or below the line, what the individual letters look like. This is hard work so don't expect much on this attempt. However bean pictures will occupy the class tomorrow until they are completed. The bean pictures go up on the bulletin board. Next the children will get strips of paper with their names printed and a space underneath where they can begin to print their names. We will remind them to copy the printed letters and to space their letters neatly. For the next few days, practicing writing our names will take up much of the class's time. When the class has developed some skill in writing, we want to hang these first attempts where all can see them. I like to create a chart titled I can write my name. As each child masters this task, they write the letters neatly on a small card that we attach to our chart. Eventually we will create a bulletin board to show the progress that the children are making. I do not hesitate to ask for "do-overs" until I get competent work for the bulletin board in the hallway—the rule being that all work going into the hallway must be "perfect." Finally, hallway work goes home to proud parents.

Writing our names is practiced continuously. When strips of paper are distributed, the teacher directs the children to write their name as it is on the name cards taped to their desks. At first these strips do not have a line at the bottom but as the children progress, we give out strips with a line drawn and they are directed to write the letters on the line.

Some children will improve so rapidly that they will write in upper- and lowercase letters after a few attempts. So the teacher needs to quickly make that chart to hang in a prominent place—titled I can write my name. When a child can reproduce first name in upper- and lowercase letters, they get a smaller card where they write their name and it is pasted onto the chart. Applause and recognition whenever a name is added to the chart. If a child has difficulty and it is illegible, it becomes a "do-over." Where it is clearly impossible, discontinue the task and have the child work (one-on-one) with an educational assistant. Children love the individual attention so the practice continues and the applause will come.

TEACHING KIDS TO READ AND WRITE—A MASTER PLAN

This is a defining moment for me. I would like to discuss the elements of *a well-integrated program* that produces literate, excited, intellectually oriented learners. It makes strenuous demands on the teacher because she or he is consistently incorporating a multitude of activities into a daily schedule. Also the teacher must know each pupil and the progress that each is making in the most concrete way. Nevertheless, the children will learn rapidly and enthusiastically. This overview of the plan will focus on three areas:

1. We must create a special *environment.*
2. We must develop specific, beneficial *routines.*
3. We must create *special events or culminating acts* to indicate progress.

Environment

The program cannot work without lots and lots of *books.* First, there must be an organized selection of books. Each school or school district usually commits to a reading system. This involves a selection of books organized around some philosophy of learning. Most schools expect teachers to adhere to a timetable that charts instruction. Class work is spread out over a unit, perhaps a module, perhaps a yearlong plan. A graded set of books will be available for each child to use individually and as part of a group. This method is called *Balanced Literacy* and we stress reading aloud, shared reading, guided, and independent reading.

AN EXCELLENT
EARLY CHILDHOOD
ENVIRONMENT

This approach uses literary materials where picture clues, inferences, language patterns, and predicting aid in reading. But in addition to books that teach the skill of reading, there must also be an extensive library of books that build up each child's knowledge base. *In addition to basic literacy, I have always stressed content, vocabulary skills, spelling, and amassing knowledge so there is increasing confidence about the world and how it works.* The Core Knowledge program of E. D. Hirsch is much like the education that I received as a child. We learned about history, art, music, geography, as well as literature and science. I believe that both "basic literacy" and "Core Knowledge" together produce the scholarly, enlightened students that I cherish, that I have produced.

In my learning lab or kindergarten classroom, we might expect to find a selection of picture books of many kinds. There will be fairy tales, stories about animals, holidays, trains, boats, airplanes, rockets, children in America and how they live but also children in other countries, folktales (the kind of stories that grandmothers tell), stories about how to solve a problem or books illustrating how to make something. There must be enough books so that children can read them in school, but also take them home over the weekend. It is important to have books about science, mathematics, ethics and values, books for singing, and books about dancing, books of poetry, a set of encyclopedias and indeed anything that might interest young children.

Together with lots of books, I expect to see *alphabet letters* posted around the room. I like them best if they are stapled low along one wall in the room. At the beginning of the year, it is helpful if each letter has a picture accompanying to illustrate the sound (a ball with letter *b*, a lamp with letter *l*, a truck with letter *t*). The pictures are helpful when children are learning phonic sounds. The fact that they are perhaps a foot from the floor allows a child to sit on the floor and work or write independently. These letters can be purchased in any teacher's store.

Another tremendously valuable tool in the classroom environment is *A Word Wall*. I love this learning tool. The best way to use a word wall is to attach blank poster boards to the wall. I like to cover seven or eight feet of space so that we are creating a huge class dictionary. A very useful resource that is valuable from kindergarten to third grade is called *Teaching Reading and Writing with Word Walls* by Janiel M. Wagstaff (1999). If the teacher chooses a "Big Book" for the week, the class will read this book daily for a week. Some special "teaching point" will be discussed each day. Words that are repeated often and begin with the phonic sounds to be learned that week go on the Word Wall. In addition to learning the sounds of alphabet letters, use of the Word Wall helps learners internalize them so well that they will be recognized automatically. Having words written correctly on the wall will facilitate correct spelling as well as clarify the use of initial and final letters in creating words.

Poems that are well loved and rhymes and "jump rope" patters offer many words that will go on the Word Wall. Children will happily chant "Miss Mary Mack" and follow the words with a pointer. The teacher can reinforce word recognition by having individual children come up to "frame" words with their hands to show that they are really reading them.

Every well-organized classroom will have a *Writing Center*. It becomes important as children begin to work independently, individually or in small groups. Ideally there will be several small tables and chairs, a paper bin, and cups holding pencils, markers (assorted colors), a stapler, and perhaps a date stamp so that each child will be able to record the date on the day's work. This Center should be somewhat removed from noisy areas (where board games like Scrabble are being played).

A Computer Center is a necessity in today's kindergartens. Even in areas thought of as disadvantaged, children have access to computers which they share with older siblings or parents. There is no reason why students with skills should not do research, write articles, write editorials, and opinion pieces as well as type up stories, play educational games involving phonics, letter identification, or vocabulary skills. Remember that today's schools as well as teachers have an obligation to teach all students computer skills. Young children will be motivated to make birthday cards and type simple greetings, write letters to students who are sick, or write letters to a parent who is not in the child's home.

ROUTINES 'ROUND READING AND WRITING

These are the daily or frequent activities integrated into the reading/writing program. The first component is a strong *phonics program*. Let me be very clear about this. I have no faith in a reading program that does not emphasize phonics, particularly when working with disadvantaged or culturally different children. It is clear to me that such children will have a difficult time writing independently and learning new words without phonetic instruction. (See pp. 48–60) In my kindergarten, I only introduce one, possibly two alphabet letters/sounds per week. We try to incorporate each new sound into the Morning Message, the homework, and the writing activities (i.e., the experience charts, seat work). Because the phonetic component is cumulative and because the children must learn all twenty-six alphabet sounds, week by week their store of letters and sounds grows. The fact that every child knows the "Alphabet Song" (to the tune of "Twinkle, Twinkle") gives a coherence to the task of learning so that they know which letter and sound comes next and they begin to anticipate. The literacy system mandated by the district will be successful if it is complemented by a solid phonics program. When I was a child, reading programs were very, very different.

We had textbooks that contained stories that were made up of a certain number of words. Book editors controlled the words, the frequency with which they appeared, and their level of difficulty. We were the "Run, Tom run," generation. Reading could be very dull. Today educators believe that the best way for children to learn to read is from children's own literature, from stories, folk songs, poems, and varied other materials. Rather than learning all words by rote, (memorizing without much thought) we now understand that children can "construct knowledge," can use skills and abilities to read, understand, and learn from reading. We now teach children to use strategies that help them to figure out words that they don't know and also to think about the story that they are reading so they can predict what will happen. As they attempt to understand the story they are learning new ways to solve problems and, most importantly, they will experience pleasure in the activity of reading.

Every day we gather on the rug for our Morning Message and Shared Reading. I like to start the day with a song and a finger play. At that time, I write the Sentence of the Day. Early in September, I begin with the sentence, "I like school." It is important for the class to learn the word *like* because we will be using it in our experience chart stories. It is introduced as a "sight" word, a heavy-duty word at that. After Morning Meeting is finished, I frequently ask the children to return to their seats and write the sentence of the day on paper strips. These go into their individual portfolio boxes. They may also copy the experience charts, or specific tasks that are assigned to groups.

It is very helpful to *divide the class into three groups*. After time on the rug, the children can copy a sentence but also engage in other writing activities. It has become a tradition in my class to have these groups—the Explorers (advanced group), the Power Rangers (intermediates), and the Chipmunks (those struggling with the basics). It tickles me that everyone wants to be a Chipmunk. This tells me that the class cannot see the basis for the divisions. Good! No hurt feelings.

I have mentioned that the time before Morning Meeting, is a *quiet reading period*. This is a routine that is crucial to reading success. As the children acquire words and can make sense of them they will be able to read story books. Some children will read the same book over and over before mastering the vocabulary. Others will pair with a friend and read to each other from the Big Book of the week. They love the Big Books because by the end of the week they know most of the words. Other children will take a story book, a book that looks appealing, or one of those small handheld books (i.e., Rigby Collection) that was introduced in small group reading. Indeed, since my assistant teacher and I read with children one-on-one all the time, these small books are taken to be savored during quiet reading time. As you can see they have so many opportunities to read, decode, and enjoy books that they slide into literacy—effortlessly.

I was the storyteller at the Hans Christian Andersen Memorial in New York's Central Park for three years. What a dream job! During the week I taught a preschool group in Murphy Playground just north of the East Village. On Saturday I would stand in an open area in front of a statue of Hans Christian Andersen and address a delightful audience of children. We began with a finger play, then I would tell three stories. The last one was always one created by the great Danish author. During the week I located and learned folktales, fairy tales, and modern stories from around the world. The tales by the Brothers Grimm were favorites. Also we enjoyed the African-based Anansi stories and the Russian and French tales that still enchant us after hundreds of years. The stories that my children loved most were about young people who overcame obstacles because they were brave, like the young boy in *Jack and the Beanstalk*, persevering and clever like Anansi the Spider, who was able to protect himself from bigger, stronger enemies because he could outsmart them. These grand stories were very important to my audience because they showed that young people could solve problems, help others in trouble and trust their own judgment in emergencies. My respect for *story time* is great. This is the time when youngsters are enriched and enchanted by verbal magic. The language of stories in books, even in its simplest forms, is the language of the adult world. Through stories they will learn more and more complex patterns of speech, more beautiful and imaginative forms of expression so that their store of language will become richer and more varied as they grow. My little ones will use these riches as they write and express their own ideas in their own stories but also on tests and essays throughout their academic careers. With luck and determination they may someday be able to use these skills as professionals, whether in the university, the office, advertising, law journals, or in creating books that others will buy in order to learn, to be transported to other worlds so that cultures different from theirs will have meaning. One of the reasons that we ask parents to read to their children daily is because we know that the words that they hear and absorb will become *their words* and give them the power to shape, change, and understand their environment throughout their lives. Words are powerful. Communication is a powerful tool. It is the kindergarten teacher's first gift.

One of my favorite routines is *naptime.* Since you must accept the notion, as a kindergarten teacher, that you rarely sit, and never rest during the day, naptime is for *them*, not for *you.* Naptime gives me the opportunity to exercise my "secret weapon." I am very serious about this. The secret of my success relates to Naptime. Why? Because it allows me to do systematic one-on-one teaching. My strategy is a regular tutorial with each child. This is why 1) I know the abilities of each child at all times and 2) why I am able to tailor lessons depending on the growth and skills of a child. Naptime is the perfect time for this individualized teaching. Think about it! The class goes to lunch and then goes to the yard for outdoor play. When they come in from racing around and playing games, they generally have a rest period. Kindergarteners, usually exhausted from the playground, will fall asleep. Those who no longer take naps might read quietly. This is the time when I call children to a small table and have them read for me. I usually start these lessons with a couple of bright kids. What I have learned over the years is that *the others listen.* Even the sleepers listen for a while before they drift off to sleep. This situation is similar to those children who were educated in one-room schoolhouses. Because there were so many age-grades, one group would recite while the others were performing some other task or quietly reading. However the situation allowed those, not being taught, to listen in on those who were. Naptime gives me the silence that I need for concentration.

My reading materials were four little pamphlets that really taught my children how to read. Or at least, convinced them that they were beginning to read. The first was called *Winter Surprise*. The second was *To Sam*. The third was *Too Many Toys*, and the fourth was *The Mitten* (Houghton Mifflin, 1991) These books had been created for independent reading.

However, they were perfect for my purposes. Here is my strategy. I would alert two or three children that I would be working with them. Forget sleep! The importance of reading with the teacher was such that they would sit, beaming, and waiting their turn. Before me were the little books and a sheet that I used to record. I used a heavy manila folder which I had divided up into boxes with a ruler. There were usually eight squares on the short side and twelve squares on the long side. I wrote children's names down the short side. When I called a child to read I wrote the name of little book we were using, the date, and a notation "1st r.", "2nd r." . . . The first time we picked up one of those little books I asked the child to guess what the story was about. The picture on the cover often contained a clue. For a very first read, I took the child's finger and we pointed to each word in the sentence as I read it. I let the child read each word next. The sentences on the following pages were similar to the first page so the child began to get the pattern. There were only a few pages so by the end of the book, the child was always flabbergasted. It was as if the student was saying, "I did it! I—I read a book." It was always a good idea to ask a few questions to make sure the child understood what the book was about. Also, just to check, I pointed to several words to make sure that the child knew each word and was not reciting from memory what he or she had heard. At this point I made a notation that this was a "1st r." or first reading. With a smile and a compliment, I sent the child back to his/her seat and beckoned to the second child to come. Each child was entitled to two or more chances to read each book. Whenever they did a perfect reading, I made a check in the box and the next time that child was called, we read a new book. Please note that in the morning on the rug, during quiet reading time, these were the books that the children delighted in reading alone or to a friend. These books went home in a Ziploc bag so that parents could see their progress and in time a chart went up on the wall. At first I wrote in the name of each book as it was read (without error), but as their writing skills developed, the children had the honor of writing themselves. My point here is that as I developed my reading program, I made sure that I read these four books with each child, individually. Sure, it is exhausting (never really boring) but the payoff is so great, the children are so happy, it is well worth the effort. Imagine the joy that a parent expresses when you let the child read for the parent/parents/caregiver that comes on Open School Night. Because they know how important reading skill is in a child's academic career, I would often see tears in my Harlem parents' eyes. Small group reading continued to be a major component of the program but I added individual reading because I found it to be the best way of introducing children to reading.

Imagine the child's reaction—the teacher's complete attention for a sustained amount of time! It is like magic!

I include *Homework* in my master plan because it has value in the reading/writing program. I am somewhat skeptical about the results of homework because homework has a positive effect only if parents are cooperative. When the parent has many children, they must be concerned about tomorrow's clothing and tonight's dinner, homework might be used incorrectly as an instrument of literacy. Homework is not a learning tool if a parent sends the child off to do an assignment with no supervision saying, "Go do your homework." This is not a recreation period for the parent. The child might need a pencil, might not understand the assignment, might have difficulty reproducing the letter, might need to be told that a "do-over" is necessary. A helping adult should always be accessible when homework is being done. And horror of horrors, parents should never do the assignment for the child. This is a regular occurrence. When I check the results the next day in school, there is frequently a page where an impatient parent has completed the assignment. Adult work looks different from a child's efforts. We struggle to make grown-ups understand that the child is learning during the homework experience. We have to monitor their activity to make sure that they are not learning incorrect patterns and yet must give them the space to work independently. It works best if we keep an eye on them and definitely check finished work, but it is important to handle this period with gentle good humor, a lot of praise and much patience. There should be an ample supply of paper so if the child wants to begin again, it is all right. Harsh criticism or ridicule has no place here. Also, parents should not be surprised if the teacher calls to inquire about missed homework. Teachers need to make them understand that homework is an important way of reinforcing what has been learned so that it is firmly fixed in the child's mind and can be called up in other situations. And lastly, daily homework is another way of teaching a child to participate in learning. We want to establish routines that help a child understand his or her responsibilities as a student so that the school's expectations are clear and the mature student gains in confidence as the school year proceeds.

Experience Charts

I love them . . . passionately. I see the pride in my children's eyes as they find their very own name on a big piece of paper . . . as they read the words they have spoken. Often after school, children bring their mommies and daddies into the classroom to read the experience chart, where they have made a contribution. In past years we have strung ropes across the classroom in all directions and hung up the experience charts so that many of them were available. We use them for everything . . . reporting on class trips, unusual weather like blizzards, all holidays, thinking-skills lessons, special assemblies, poems that we like, songs that are fun or serious songs like "My Country, 'Tis of Thee," that the class needs to know for assemblies and special events, and short biographical sketches of notable people. One of my favorite things is to give outdated experience charts to children to take home as a reward for academic progress. In the classroom, everything is read and reread by everyone.

And we keep pointers and rulers available so that during Discovery Time and Choice Time, children can read to each other or indeed read silently for the pleasure of it. Even when they have memorized the material, constant exposure to the words causes them to be added to the child's vocabulary. See pages 35, 40–44 for examples.

CULMINATING EVENTS

The educators at Columbia University were the first people that I heard use the term "to celebrate." They celebrated Units completed, important learning . . . any kind of summing up activity. The notion of recognizing "completions" is a powerful one, particularly as a source of pride as *children reflect* on what they have done and as a mechanism for *remembering information.* Taking home something to show Grandma is a terrific way to show learning but it is only one way to motivate children. Another way to motivate children to struggle on in the difficult process of learning to read and write is to give them chances to show what they can do. In other words, we periodically celebrate the milestones of their development.

1. What a joy it is when a child brings a book to read to the class. Early in the year it may be a favorite that the child has shared many times with a parent or babysitter or relative. It may be partially memorized. We applaud the effort. But a giant step has been taken when the child points to each word and reads.

2. When the children are advanced enough to write their own stories we always have a "sharing time" or conference when some are selected to read and some volunteer. We hold the paper up so it can be seen and the child points to

each word and reads the story. The proud reader sits in the "author's chair" beside the teacher and graciously accepts the applause of classmates (a proud moment for any child). By springtime, children read and write so well that we send them to other classes to inspire others.

3. During lunchtime I make deals with other teachers (these are generally good friends). At an agreed-upon hour my child and an educational assistant goes to another class to read a story. We keep the story short. It is generally a crowd-pleaser that my kids enjoy. It is especially delightful if the child visits a class where an older sibling can say, "That's my baby sister." (We have also had the curious situation where my kid reads with more fluency than an older sibling. Tactfully, we do not visit.)

4. We celebrate the growing skill of a child when he/she can read a story without error. That book goes home in a Ziploc bag so parents can really be proud. Please remember that I said that after the student has read the fourth small book, *The Mitten*, we allow the book to go home. Now while books routinely go home over the weekend so families can share in the child's reading development, the celebration of a book that has been read is treated differently. There is a chart where the child writes the name of the book beside his name and there is room for twenty four additions.

5. The teacher always has a supply of small blank books for those who want to write and illustrate their own books. Children love to give these as presents on holidays or birthdays.

6. The class produces several Big Books after trips or special events. With these books one child may write text while another can draw the picture. Both sign their names on the page.

7. It doesn't happen often but sometimes we have children who are so gifted that they are able to plan and execute an entire bulletin board of their own work. They may have six or seven stories of which they are quite proud. We let them decorate

the board, choose a title for the display, and I make a sign introducing the child to the school. Believe me, parents come in to take pictures of the child and the bulletin board.

8. Our school has a Multicultural Fair in the spring. This is a culminating event for all the classes in our school. It is a fitting time to show all the class storybooks and individual projects that have been produced by the class. One year my class produced a set of posters with a picture and a short essay on the topic—the central problem of a favorite story. In addition to writing they had to think critically. The products were outstanding and we were all very proud.

By Malcom
PLez. MoMMy, an
you give me a Kiss
befor bed time.
I Love you and Kisss
Makes Me Go to
Step I Love you

Tyrannosurus rex Eats meat.
Allosaurus EAts meat to.
Brontosaurus Eat The Tree Levs.
Protoceratops EAts The Tree Levs.
Ornitholestes EAts meat
Triceratops EAts Levs.
Stegosaurus EAts Levs.

Name: Steven   Date: May

The Taxi Dog was a pet to a Taxi man And he was hungry and lost. Thin a Taxi stopt by and took him home And meet a clown.

"Meanies" The
Story is About
Meanies. I Like
The Story.
because It is
Funny. MY
favorite Book is
"Meanies". It is a
book and The
Meanies. do
bad things.

Name Janay   Date 20 03

This Story is about
Madeline's Christmas
Madeliner Was Taking
care OF sick children.
oS She called The hospital
and The hospital came
To MissClavel.

Name: Delroy Date: **May**

This story is about Ben's dad. I like to read the story. Ben was going home with his dad. His dad was a sailor.

6

Masterly Teaching

I OFTEN THINK THAT teaching is an art masquerading as a science. Pedagogy is its scientific name. And like other arts, successful teaching demands concrete skills that must be learned. Just as a landscape artist must calculate lines of perspective, and a painter must understand the relationship of one color to another and has a better chance of capturing a likeness, when painting a human face, if principles of anatomy are understood, the classroom teacher will be successful when a repertoire of skills are in place. A teacher can learn to plan, experiment, research a subject (as can an artist). Yet a great teacher and a great artist both have qualities that are not subject to analysis. They can both create magic. This is easy to see when examining a Rembrandt or a Leonardo da Vinci. One can only stare in amazement at the subtlety of color, the beauty of form, (in Rembrandt, the sense of suffering in an old man's face). The viewer understands that we are seeing something unique; we are looking at something rare. A master teacher can evoke that same sense of awe, when ideas fall into place, when the listener stops breathing for a moment, and rides a wave of pleasure and understanding to a new place, a new level of awareness that is thrilling. Often master teachers can take complex concepts like *intelligence* or *time* or *authority* and make them comprehensible. Suddenly the listener understands what was formerly murky and unclear. This new understanding can be plugged into a larger system and all of a sudden generalities, even laws become accessible.

Well then, are master teachers born or can they be taught? I believe that master teachers can be developed. If administrators and those who train teachers made it a goal of staff development, I believe that more teachers would achieve this status as they evolve and grow in teaching. Let me suggest some characteristics that are connected with the exalted status . . . master teacher.

FIRST OF ALL, MASTER TEACHERS ENJOY WHAT THEY DO.

There is an ease that comes when the teacher understands the task so well that it is communicated with pleasure. And that pleasure comes from a sound knowledge and understanding of the information to be imparted. For example, the teacher must teach phonics to each incoming kindergarten class year after year. Because the teacher has developed a set of lessons that describe each alphabet letter in great detail, it is possible to sail into this instructional unit confident that by June, the children will have mastered the material. An illustration of the expertise involved can be seen in learning the sound of the letter *m*. I introduce the letter to the children as part of a writing lesson. After presenting the "lowercase" letter and making the sound, I give examples of words that begin with the *m* sound like *mother* or *milk* or *marshmallow*.

These are powerful words to a child. They have psychological associations or remind the children of things they like to taste. Because these words are an intimate part of a child's world, the words and sounds that begin them will be easy to remember. Suppose I said *metal* or *measure* or *monstrous*, these words have the correct sounds but don't conjure up familiar and emotion-laden objects. While I continue to repeat the sound of *m* I understand that the auditory experience is more powerful if it is supplemented by tactile and visual experience. So next I have the children draw the letter in the air three or four times. As they write in the air, I singsong as I write the letter with them and describe the strokes they must make. I say, "Down, up and down, up and down. What is the sound of the letter *m*?" Next we must all write the letter several times. Also, I will hold up toys and pictures of objects that begin with the *m* sound. The homework for the day will contain practice in writing the letter and drawing objects with that sound. Future drills and classroom exercises will cement this learning. It is significant that after twenty years of teaching phonics this way, I still sail into the unit with enthusiasm. Perhaps this is because I understand what the children are getting. For disadvantaged children, knowledge of phonics is the key to success in reading. Therefore, I enjoy teaching this curriculum. The more I teach it, the easier it is to teach. Imagine my satisfaction as I see four- and five-year-olds internalizing the letters and beginning to write them down, later writing words. A touching moment occurred one day as an African American mother began to cry as her child pointed to words and said them. "My baby's reading," she whispered.

MASTER TEACHERS DISPLAY UNUSUAL COMMUNICATION SKILLS.

I have said that they can make complex ideas simple. No mean ability! But they can do much more. Master teachers can paint pictures with words. They can stir the imagination. Think of someone who can tell stories using a rich vocabulary and who can make students feel and travel to another place imaginatively or make time stand still for a moment. This can happen in a kindergarten class during story hour as well as in a college lecture hall.

Master teachers can create "teachable moments." These wonderful situations occur when, in the midst of a lesson, a child says something surprising. The child takes something that he or she has learned and hooks it onto something that has been remembered or seen somewhere. Perhaps all of the class will jump in and make further observations. Maybe a few don't understand but they are focused and listening with interest. At that moment, the teacher takes the child's insight and moves the discussion to another level. It is crucial that the teacher seize the moment, recognize how important it is and run with it. Chances are that a similar moment will not come again. It is a "hot" moment, when something remarkable has happened. How to handle it? I could take a "Post-it" and remind myself to take up this subject at a later time. After all, now it is math time. I might want to postpone more discussion because I might want to find a chart that illustrates this point or I might want to devote a whole new unit to this subject (the child's comment tells me that the class might be ready for this new material). However, I believe that these "teachable moments" need to be recognized and built on immediately. A door has opened and some of the children are ready to leap through. Although some don't understand what has happened, it is not a lost moment for them. They see that others are responding so it is a "shaping" moment, where they are *motivated* to know, though they don't yet understand.

A novice teacher might not recognize what is happening, might not know how to mine the situation for the valuable learning that is possible. A master teacher delays the math lesson and offers the class new learnings, information, and insights. There are many teachable moments. They happen all the time. My point is that these are moments of great power where children can make great leaps of understanding.

Let me illustrate a teachable moment that did not result from a child's insight but from a recording that made a difficult concept clearer. I had talked to my children about Martin Luther King, Jr. and his early years in Atlanta, but discrimination is a difficult concept for five-year-olds. It is easier to talk about black and white children being unable to go to school together or Rosa Parks on the bus and the significance of her courageous stand. However one day I put the "I Have a Dream" speech on the phonograph. The children heard the shouts of the crowd and the intensity and power of Dr. King's words. There is a rising excitement as he speaks and the audience is pulled along emotionally. Dr. King talks about the fact that someday little black and white children will hold hands together. When he ends with "Free at last! Thank God Almighty, we are free at last!" My kindergarteners jumped to their feet, clapping, and shouting. Here was my "teachable moment." They understood the situation more clearly now and had a sense of its importance. They heard the shouts of thousands, felt sympathy for school children like themselves (after all, we had black and Hispanic children in our class). They saw Dr. King as someone who was there to help. (I was appalled to learn that all of them knew that he had been shot.) But imagine the teaching and learning that went on after they heard the speech. They had felt the power that a leader can have on a multitude. Dr. King was helping to change a bad situation. Incidentally, they memorized the last part of the speech and recited it in assembly in January.

These wonderful "teachable moments," when understandings crystallize in new ways, are very important. They come most frequently to "master teachers." These are educators who are very skilled, who generally have years and years of experience and who feel like high-level professionals. I am aware that some individuals in the profession are alarmed by any distinctions that categorize teachers based on merit. They want a democratic leveling that causes all teachers to be treated equally (particularly financially) so they discourage distinctions. However it is necessary to point out that school teaching is perhaps the only profession that does not routinely reward outstanding ability with financial mobility (i.e., merit pay). This is certainly untrue at higher levels. In the university, "crackerjack" teachers and researchers are lured away from one institution to another by hefty raises in salary, quality housing, and other amenities.

Master teachers are frequently discussed in literature. In his valuable book, *Great Teachers*, Houston Peterson (1946) compiled a number of essays that were written by the admirers of distinguished educators or by their grateful students. He develops a portrait of Mark Hopkins, a legendary professor of philosophy at Williams College for over fifty years. In his essay on Hopkins, Leverett Wilson Spring is impressed by several personal qualities of this charismatic man. We should not be surprised that one of them is Hopkins' capacity for *enthusiasm*. However, here it is described differently. Great teachers like Hopkins have a kind of passion for the subject that they teach. They radiate an excitement that touches the hearts and minds of their students who are changed in significant ways. In later years they still recognize their experience in the classroom of their mentor as a "defining moment" in their lives. The desire to read more, know more grows over time, so that unexpected career choices result.

Spring compared this enthusiasm of Hopkins to the incandescence of certain religious leaders. The passion and commitment in his lectures actually had a "spiritual" dimension. But there is something else.

MASTER TEACHERS HAVE A THOROUGH AND WIDE-RANGING KNOWLEDGE OF THE SUBJECT THEY TEACH.

Their great interest has caused them to learn as much as they could so they are comfortable when students ask questions. Where answers are still unknown, they can indicate promising lines of inquiry that are being investigated. Such teachers are always researchers aware of current ideas that are being discussed in their areas of specialization. For example, a master teacher in the field of early childhood education would be aware of current research going on in schools of education about how young children learn, about effective methods of helping children with learning deficits, about creating environments in which children can learn successfully, about handling problems of behavior, attention and peer group interaction (i.e., fighting, listening, settling disputes). Such an accomplished person would be sure to know how to set up a classroom, how to teach a lesson, how to encourage parents, how to plan units of study for the class. This is a superb professional.

MASTER TEACHERS FIND WAYS TO BE CREATIVE IN ORDER TO BE EFFECTIVE.

I respond to the artistic possibilities of classroom teaching as day after day I solve problems. An effective teacher soon learns the strengths and weaknesses of each child, then develops activities that facilitate learning. If Sara has trouble remembering the difference between *b* and *d* I can quickly sketch a picture of a book, a separate picture of a dog then roll out the Play-Doh. The playtime fun of making alphabet letters and grouping them with the correct pictures can solve a recognition problem and help to remember the phonic sounds.

There are so many ways that I can teach, develop the "cultural capital" of my children while I am also stimulated artistically. I love fairy tales and folktales. My repertoire grows as I collect stories to tell the class so they can learn about other cultures a well as their own. I can play the piano (there was a time when kindergarten teachers had to show skill on the piano in order to be certified) for skipping or dancing, but when my children are resting, they listen to classical music or jazz. We *discuss* music; they learn to request pieces that they enjoy. They learn the difference between a Mozart concerto and a march by Elgar ("Pomp and Circumstance").

One of my favorite activities is mural-making. I latched on to this art form as I read about the "infant schools" in New Zealand. There the children paint complicated environments (a patterned Maori design) or a neighborhood scene as a backdrop for their stories or little essays. These murals can be six or seven feet long. They are very beautiful and the children are highly motivated to write and decorate them.

Another activity that teacher and children enjoy is the creation of extravaganzas for assemblies. Assemblies are extremely important in the lives of school children. Besides the demands of decorum, where children learn to sit quietly for a period of time, assembly period is of immense value in teaching values related to citizenship (the Pledge of Allegiance, the national anthem, songs that have captured the imagination of the country like "We are the World," patriotic songs as well as songs that bind us together like Disney's

"It's a Small World"). With so many immigrant children coming from so many countries to live in the United States, assemblies are a fine way to impart cultural forms that we consider important. They can learn about holidays that Americans celebrate, important figures in our history, cultural forms like square dancing, the folk music and tales of Native Americans, the songs and customs of the regions in America (i.e., the West, the South). They can celebrate Women's History Month. What better way to teach children, who come from countries where women have low status that in our country we struggle to see that women and men are treated with the same respect. Black History Month, Hispanic Heritage Month, Dr. King's birthday, and Saint Patrick's Day, give the school the chance to emphasize the contributions of the many ethnic groups that live and work in this society. One of my favorite memories of teaching is our multicultural assembly. In my Harlem school we did an African dance (with drums) to "Everybody Loves Saturday Night" from Ghana, a Puerto Rican song "El Coquito," a song with French phrases called, "French Is Really Easy after All." At the end we held hands and recited a song that Paul Robeson made famous:

THE HOUSE I LIVE IN
RECORDED BY: EARL ROBINSON
LYRICS BY: ABEL MEEROPOL

The house I live in,
A plot of earth, a street,
The grocer and the butcher,
And the people that I meet;
The children in the playground,
The faces that I see
All races, all religions,
That's America to me.

A colleague reminded me of the lasting influence of master teachers when she called to tell me of an encounter with a student of mine on a bus. This young lady, whom I will call Keyana Reeves, had been in an enrichment club that I formed in my school. I was well aware of the academic ability of some of my kindergarteners who were now in fourth and fifth grade. One year they were so brilliant that I decided to follow them from kindergarten to first grade. Keyana was one of those super-bright kids. So I went to the upper grade teachers and asked them to permit me to form an enrichment group where I could do advanced work with extremely able students. My area of interest was the arts and culture of Ancient Egypt. We were to meet once weekly during lunch where films, discussions, projects, field trips (i.e., the Temple of Dendur at the Metropolitan Museum of Art) would introduce them to Egyptology, a field that they could build on in future years. Keyana was one of nine students who worked with me over two years.

We looked at wonderful videos of historical sites like the pyramids, the opening of the tomb of Tutankhamen. We read a novel, *The Egypt Game.* (Snyder, 1967) We discussed the pantheon of Egyptian gods, the climate and geology of Egypt, the religious beliefs of these ancient people. What the students learned was apparent as they prepared bulletin boards (with essays) for inspection and exhibits for our annual district-wide multicultural fair (Tut's sarcophagus or coffin, writing our names using the symbols that they used, called hieroglyphics, a model of an Egyptian house). Of course they used the library and read many books to complete their essays that accompanied the artifacts.

The writing skill of the students improved so significantly that I began thinking of a way to show them off to their parents and others. I decided to enter them in an essay contest sponsored by the Manhattan borough president's office during Women's History Month. While I suspect that not many schools participate in a competition like this and further, I suspect that every well-written, thoughtful piece becomes a winner, all of our entrants were winners. We went to city hall where we were part of a public ceremony, where each student was presented with a gold medal on a multicolored ribbon to be worn around the neck (like winners in the Olympics). The then Borough President, C. Virginia Fields, actually read the essay of one of my students to the audience of proud parents and glowing students. Our principal recognized their achievement by congratulating them over the loudspeaker and then let me take them from class to class where they were praised.

7

Authority—Encouraging Self-control

NEW TEACHERS, ESPECIALLY THOSE in schools where reading scores are very low, face a daunting experience. They must enter a strange classroom with very little preparation and face a roomful of strange children, many of whom are immediately hostile. It is difficult to understand the probing for weakness, the explosive jeering, and outbreaks of fighting and bullying that occur precisely because there is a new person on the scene. If the teacher is brought into the room by an assistant principal or other supervisor, is formally introduced to the class and clear demands for correct behavior are made, the class may be orderly and quiet for a while. But soon enough it will start. "Teacher, can I go to the bathroom?" or "My brother has my notebook. I need the pass to go to his classroom and get it." While jockeying for the pass begins, and some pushing, shoving, hats, and other missiles begin to fly through the air, and the noise level rises, some children will be sitting quietly, watching the new teacher intently. A few of them will continue to be cooperative, well aware of parental expectations. However, some are quiet while they size the newcomer up. Is he or she getting rattled? Looking startled or beginning to look angry? Often the most difficult students are quiet. Their motivations are complex. If they are "known offenders" and have been the recipients of teacher telephone calls, guidance reports, even suspensions, these children are making quiet decisions. They may be saying *This teacher does not know me. Maybe I can "chill" and stay out of trouble this time.* Unfortunately sometimes the rage that is just below the surface can be triggered by almost anything so that, soon enough, there will be an incident.

As an experienced or "master teacher" used to difficult populations I can suggest alternative strategies that may calm the situation. The first is that no one goes to the bathroom for the first hour. Later maybe. Next, I have to become a "known quantity," one that they can respect. When I am beginning a new year with a class on the first day I like to take time to tell them about myself. For a few moments I talk about where I was born (Alabama) the schools I attended in Brooklyn, Manhattan, and Queens. A teacher who has had a disadvantaged background should certainly talk about it. For example, the teacher could say, "I grew up right down the street on 110th Street." "Like many of you, I grew up in 'the projects'" or "I remember eating in the lunchroom. It wasn't so nice then. They only gave us soup and a sandwich." I do not linger on the past but quickly outline the things that I intend to do with the class during the year. I want them to understand that many events will be pleasant. I always take three trips with kindergarteners. They are usually the American Museum of Natural History, the aquarium and the zoo. Because I spend a lot of time socializing my kids so that they are well behaved outside the classroom, I will consider other trips as well. But I always warn them that I do not take disruptive youngsters on trips.

I mean this. "Going on trips" can be a terrific motivational tool that helps difficult children to shape up. When they have been left behind even once, it leads to a reevaluation of the classroom experience. (I am quick to tell a parent that I cannot be responsible for Ronald because he is too aggressive and we will be on public transportation. I will relent only if the parent accompanies the child on the trip.)

It is important for students to understand that I have the power to influence them and their behavior. Within the first week of school, they must recognize that there is a set of standards determining their behavior. With prompting from me, we will draft a code of behavior or Class Rules to be mounted on the wall. I constantly refer to it when there are problems. And yet at the same time, I want them to realize that we are going to have lots of fun. For example, all birthdays will be celebrated. There will be holiday parties with parental cooperation. My special promise is that we will have special movies and "eats" every Friday. My class works so hard all week that by Friday we are all ready to "kick back" and "hang loose." Sometimes it is a video or a great story with a long pretzel (lying on the rug).

My authority (my power to influence them and their behavior) is revealed in the strategies that I have access to, the understandings that underlie my supervision in the classroom, and a coolness of demeanor suggests that nothing is going to surprise me or deter me from my goal of leading the class and teaching the lesson. So let me share some insights about *behavior*:

1. Young children "test" new personnel to find out if the newcomer can provide them with a safe environment. If they cannot control themselves, can you? Can you protect them from aggressive classmates? If dangerous events occur, can you protect them? They do not relax until they are sure of your competence. Sometimes a matter-of-fact, calm handling of routines gives them the assurance that they need.

2. Senior teachers always tell newcomers. And newcomers seldom listen. When you say that you are going to do something, do it. The security that young children feel is bound up in recognizing that the teacher keeps her/his word. Consistency is key. You are on a "slippery slope" if you allow yourself to be charmed out of a "time-out" by Byron's assurance

that he will never, ever drop sunflower seeds down Kareem's collar again during assembly. If you have indicated that deviations in assembly will not be tolerated, Byron's charm is to be ignored. If you indicate that a letter to Mom is going home today, make sure that it does. (Also leave a space and indicate that Mom or a caregiver must sign to show that the note has been read.) Then it is returned to the teacher.

3. Safety and decorum outside the classroom are of major importance. Assemblies and public gatherings are situations where cooperation and good manners must be expected. Children must learn to listen quietly and show respect when the principal is speaking or when a performance is under way. As a teacher, you are judged by your peers as to your skill in controlling your class. No teacher will want to take trips with you and your unruly children, so make sure that cooperation is learned early in the year. How? Practice, practice, practice . . . I have watched teachers devoting much time and attention to one child, while the rest wiggle, rock, and roll down the hallway. The extraordinary attention to one while the others cavort tells me that the teacher is really unable to control the rest. Experienced teachers make time to practice routines over and over until they are learned. There is nothing wrong with saying, "WE ARE GOING TO DO THIS UNTIL YOU WALK QUIETLY IN THE HALLWAY!" After several tries, they realize that you mean what you say, and they calm down. My class has been taken into the auditorium when no one is there to practice sitting quietly. They have been seen walking up and down the stairs during September until quiet behavior is learned. (Remember, the teacher is at the back of the line with capable monitors at the front. If the class is disturbing other classes, say loudly, "We are going to practice until you do it correctly." Senior teachers merely sigh and close their doors . . . but they understand . . . and they respect your show of authority.

4. When conducting lessons on the rug or at the chalkboard, I have those who cause problems nearby. At a moment when they are sitting quietly, comment on it. "Is everybody ready to learn? Look at Jackie! He is so mature now. His hands are quiet; his eyes are on me. He's ready. Are you?" I also feel comfortable in changing children's places when they are inattentive, moving them closer to me. When there is fighting, I stop the lesson. I approach the aggressor, take his/her hands in mine, and say something like "These hands are for writing and drawing and playing ball. They are never for fighting. Take a "time-out" and look at the Rules Chart. Go! (Time-outs should never be long because separation from the group is painful to most children. Tell the child that the time-out will be, for example, ten minutes.)

5. I can remember the situation of a teacher with a seriously injured child who had been struck on the head with a long block by a child who yelled "I am the Terminator." While it's clear that the aggressor was acting out something seen from the movies in the context of a fantasy it's also clear that a "time-out" would not suffice. It is necessary to contact the principal, the guidance office, and possibly the police. Physically violent kindergarteners are a daily occurrence these days. For the past few years we have developed a separate room and personnel who will come in to the class and take a violent child to a different location for a while, so that a parent can be contacted or order can be restored to a classroom. The teacher calls for assistance by telephone. A book or an appropriate work sheet is given to the child so that learning may continue in the special location.

6. It is crucial to document antisocial behavior. Some teachers grab a "Post-it" to jot the date, time, and a few words so the incident will not be forgotten. The note can be attached to a plan book, a clip board, or desk with the understanding that such incidents will be written up in detail later. These accounts can be used for anecdotal records, for guidance

consultations, for meetings with parents, principals or the police. Do not depend on your memory. Also other children who have witnessed an event can be helpful. If something has happened in the playground during lunch, I try to write down the witness's own words. This is particularly valuable in accident reports.

7. In shaping the behavior of children. It is useful to compliment them if possible but let them know how they are progressing. I will warn children that parents will be notified if their behavior does not improve. A telephone call can be made to the home (although disconnected phones are quite common). If they are available by phone, it is useful to talk about unacceptable behavior on the same day that the problem occurred. I also like to invite parents to come and sit in the room to observe their child. A conference later is helpful to the adult, where I can make suggestions about ways to alter behavior. I do not get upset if a parent or caregiver argues with me. They have a right to defend their child. However, I always come to a conference with a list of infractions, also dates and times. Parents in denial begin to look at the problem differently as I read from my list. Regarding bullying or physical aggression, you may be sure a child who has a grievance will rush over to tell the parent what their child has done. At the end of a conference, I often create a sheet with spaces for the five days of the week. The plan is to comment on the child's behavior for the next week (in writing) at the end of each day. Parents must sign to show that they have read the report. Sometimes it is wise to give the sheet to an older sibling to take home. In any case, I try to have something positive to say (I was pleased to see that Aida sat quietly during story time and did not touch the children nearby. However, I am sad that she forgets to use words when she is angry and hits instead. Please explain to her that we use words when we are upset.).

8. Here's some sound advice. Find out who the strong teachers are on your grade (master teachers). Throw yourself at their feet if you must but make sure that they take you under their wing. It is very important to be able to get advice when it is needed. A fellow teacher is a better choice. No need to show your limitations to the assistant principal unnecessarily. Supervisors think highly of teachers who handle situations successfully and leave them to manage the major crises that continually arise. Buddy teachers, who have effective class-room skills, are usually flattered to be mentors because people with expertise take pride in what they can do and don't mind sharing. A new teacher will learn a lot by a) having lunch with a master teacher. Come with questions. Discuss management skills but also room arrangement schedules, goals for the year, written motivations for lesson plans . . . anything that you are unsure of, b) Ask if you can sit in the senior teacher's room dur-ing one of your preparation periods. Make sure you take notes.

9. Because life is *not* fair, you may find that one year all of the disruptive children really have been put in your class. I can remember an administrator who loaded all the diffi-cult children on one or two teachers because she wanted to have one orderly classroom to show to visitors at any hour of the day. Believe me, they do not understand the word "fair." They do understand the words "unannounced visit from the district office." But wily teachers figure out ways to protect their sanity. During those horrendous years when I had six or seven very disruptive children, a friendly second grade teacher would agree to keep one on an especially difficult day so that we could have an unstressful reading period. A couple of second graders would come and escort my kid to their class and later return the child to me.

10. It's really true! If you are a new teacher you cannot "wing" it. On days when you are unprepared, crises will occur, fights will break out, and the pupils of absent teachers will be sent to *your* room. The first year of a new job demands *total*

concentration because there will be lots of stress. You must do those lesson plans conscientiously. You must keep early hours and get plenty of rest. My best advice is the following: Go into the classroom every day prepared to make the same demands. I have told new kindergarten teachers that you will find yourself saying the same things over and over (i.e., "Use words," "Walk in the hallway," "Whisper in the hallway"). Apparently on the fifty-first repetition, it sinks in, and little Maleek responds correctly. Don't count . . . but also don't be surprised at the length of time that it takes.

11. When a crisis is brewing, if I think that I'm losing control, if the noise level gets too high and I can no longer hear my own voice, there are several ways to assert my authority. Often I start a finger play. My favorite one for quieting the class always works. I didn't make it up; I have been doing it forever. This is my gift to all kindergarten teachers:

> *On my head my hands I place. On my shoulders, on my face. On my hips and at my side. Then behind me they will hide. I will hold them up so high. Quickly make my fingers fly. Hold them up in front of me. Quickly clap—one, two, three.*

If I am returning from a preparation period and the "covering" teacher has lost control and children are running around the room, I go to the light switch and cut off most of the lights. The idea is to dramatically darken the room. Then I say, "Heads down on tables, one, two, three." I wait for everybody to return to his or her seat. Things calm down in the darkened room, so I might begin to softly sing a song that we all like or make up a song for the occasion.

(TO THE TUNE OF "THE FARMER IN THE DELL")

I like a quiet class

I like a quiet class

Hi-ho, the dairy-o!

I like a quiet class.

It doesn't pay to risk further disorder, so I move to the next activity, perhaps calling each table by number, to the rug. However, I will take a moment to talk about proper behavior when I am on a preparation period. If I can get information quickly from the "covering" teacher, I will send a note home that day to the parents of the disruptive children. It is necessary, for any teacher controlling your class in your absence, to know that you are prepared to back him/her up. I expect my children to be cooperative with all school personnel. I should not be the only one that they will listen to. It is a reflection on me when they are disrespectful to others. This is an attitude that all teachers should take. It is particularly significant in the case of novice teachers, who are learning their craft. Substitute teachers and "covering" teachers should not be tortured and humiliated by small children (or by older ones, either) as they struggle to gain confidence within the culture of the school. No wonder we have so much trouble retaining teachers!

12. It never fails to amaze me. Kids love stickers. They appreciate recognition and praise. But they love stickers. They are proud to show them to their parents. I also think that stickers have an aesthetic appeal. Stickers are often beautiful and iridescent with charming colors. I enjoy giving them out and make a special attempt to find and purchase unusual stickers. I have learned that it is a good idea to show them to the class at the beginning of the school day. The notion of reward helps to shape the children's behavior in positive ways. Such positive reinforcements have value. But they are only valuable if many kinds of rewards are available. Don't underestimate the pleasure that a child gets from the comment "Good job," or a smile or spontaneous applause from the class. All of these make a student feel valued. Comments,

applause, smiles—these are intrinsic rewards and frankly, I believe them to be the most important, because they go to the heart. They give pleasure and help to shape character and disposition within. Our capabilities are aroused, and we are pushed toward expansion and development of self. A sticker is an example of an extrinsic reward, a physical object or thing that is given. It is more casual and exterior. Praise warms us within. A sticker pleases us. In the case of four- and five-year-olds, the sticker may be thought of as a first step.

8

Kids Out of Control—
Kindergarten Rage

A SURPRISING ARTICLE IN *The New York Times* identified the problem. A study by the Yale Child Study Center indicated that 5,000 prekindergarten children actually get expelled from school and are sent home annually (T. Lewin, "Research Finds a High Rate of Expulsions in Preschool," *The New York Times*, May 17, 2005, p. A12). America may have been surprised by this information, but I was not. This is because these very children will return to kindergarten in a year and add many white hairs to their teachers' heads. The regulations say that children who pose a real danger to their peers can be sent home until they are six years old. And such children really do exist although they may be only four or five years old. Let me give an example. When I was teaching in the Bronx, we welcomed a handsome African American child into our class. One boy expressed a desire to be his friend and went to stand next to him. Some little girls went over to pat him and tell him their names. I crossed the room to the library corner to get the book that I intended to read during Story Hour, when I heard a scream. I turned to see the new boy, who had snatched up a yardstick and was brandishing it like a baseball bat. He hit one child on the back and another on the head. As I dropped the book and ran to protect my children, I yelled over my shoulder to my office monitor, "Quick, get Ms. Rankin." The kid grabbed the pass and ran out the door while I sprinted across the room as he whacked another child on the shoulder. He never spoke but was smiling and appeared to be enjoying himself. As he struggled with me and managed to hit another child, Ms. Rankin entered the room and between the two of us, we disarmed him. He was thin but strong and he had actually managed to whack me although I was so angry I didn't feel it. While my supervisor literally dragged the child out of the room, I gathered my screaming class together to check for injuries and calm them after a traumatic event. After a conference with his mother the next morning, this child was immediately expelled. We later found out that he was making the rounds of the schools in our district, being expelled from each one.

Last year I documented the behavior of a Harlem kindergartener which led to his suspension early in the year. The careless violence of this child made him dangerous. And I'll tell you something . . . the other children in the class were aware that a line has been crossed, that they were not safe. Things came to a head on the jungle gym in the playground. The children were climbing up the rungs to take turns sliding down. Because the slide was part of a system of challenges (ropes, funnels, hand over hand gymnastic equipment) there was a little platform high in the air where two children could stand before launching themselves in one direction or another. Little Joey was behind Kerry, but she wasn't moving fast enough for him. She was holding on to the iron supports and looking nervous, probably gathering her courage for the long slide down. Joey started yelling at her and moved toward her. I couldn't believe my eyes. He pushed her off the platform, out into space. As she fell to the ground, she landed on the assistant teacher, who broke her fall and cradled her to the ground. Let me tell you how serious this was. The kindergartners were in the upper-grade playground because workmen were repairing equipment in the little children's yard. It could have been a fatality. After pushing her, Joey slid down. He did not even look to see what had happened to the other child, showed no remorse, and circled around for another slide.

I had already begun developing an anecdotal history of Joey's progress because he disrupted my class from the first day. In the midst of a lesson, he would jump up and run around the class. He appeared to want to be chased. When angry he would try to hit or kick the teachers. When I took his hand to prevent him from running, he would try to hit any child unlucky enough to be near him. Every morning as we conferred with his mother, he promised to be cooperative but before she had left the building, he had done something unacceptable. I discovered that he liked to be praised, seemed proud to be chosen as a leader or given a treat. But the moment he was rewarded, he reverted to negative behavior. Joey was physically and verbally abusive to the teachers. He had few academic skills, was unable to work independently, and was unable to complete assignments at his seat. I reported his behavior to the assistant principal each day.

It was necessary to isolate him from the other children because his way of interacting with them was to hit or kick. When the class was moving the teacher held his hand. In the classroom, the educational assistant sat with him and worked with him (i.e., teaching him to write his name). After a series of hearing and vision tests, after I had compiled a report documenting his continuing violence to other children, the crisis intervention team repeatedly removed him from the class. (He would often throw blocks at the children, crawl under the desks during a lesson or call out at random moments when the teacher was talking—he was not talking, but instead he was making loud noises and shouting. At this point he would be removed from the classroom.) Eventually he was evaluated by a team of professionals, among them a psychologist and a social worker, and he was removed from our school and put in a special education setting.

It is significant to me that his classmates did not like Joey. Most of his classmates were terrified of him. Even very difficult children often have a pal or a friend from the neighborhood that they can play with in the yard. But no one wanted to walk with him or hold his hand. The little girls would cry and some boys would flatly refuse. Other tough customers would prepare for battle. If he raised his hand to hit, they were prepared to take him on.

Because I had a reputation for being a "strong" teacher, I could have four or five disruptive children at any one time. And the assistant principal would sometimes open my door and shove a child into the room, saying that a teacher was absent that day and she was giving me a "helper." Worse yet, the AP would have a conference with me to tell me that some child (male or female) was creating so much havoc in someone else's room that the principal had decided to give him or her to me, convinced that with my skills, I could affect a change of behavior. Unfortunately, this is not the kind of offer that you can refuse. When teachers cannot control their classes, because they are new and have not mastered classroom routines or because they don't have success in classroom instruction, we have to pull together in the interests of school safety and equilibrium.

The biggest challenge that I have had in recent years was a brilliant youngster whom we shall call Henry. He was capable of imaginative insights and verbal skill but he had no impulse control. He was with me all year and what a stressful year it was. My first entry in my anecdotal records was October 30th. I was seeing Henry's mother and father daily to report about escalating problems. At the same time I was aware that his parents were contributing to his problems. Henry's mother was a quiet, passive woman, who talked to him in a quiet reasonable way. He was attentive until she was gone. One reason for his attention was the presence of his father. Henry was listening to his mother but was looking at his father. The child was rigid; only his eyes moved. His father, a tall, thin man, contributed to the conversation, also asking Henry to listen to the teacher and control himself, but father smelled strongly of liquor, on more than one occasion.

Invariably, his parents would leave and my troubles would begin. I could almost feel the rage in the child. I quickly learned to go to him and pull him to me for a hug, otherwise, he would lose control. At such times it was important to isolate him from the class. My records of his behavior are painful to read:

- When the children were hanging up their coats, then going to the meeting area, Henry was seen kicking John in the back.
- On line, Henry hit Joseph in the face.
- As the class walked quietly to the bathroom, Henry whistled, jumped up and down, and clapped his hands in the hallway.
- On line for lunch, Henry punched Tony in the stomach.

In keeping anecdotal records, teachers are asked to describe behavior without comment. Evaluative comments are presented elsewhere.

My efforts to change Henry's antisocial behavior began from the first day. I quickly changed his seat so he would not be near the children that he had begun bullying. It was important for me to develop a code of behavior that I could point to, to remind Henry that his actions were unacceptable. Within the first week of school, at Class Meeting, we discussed acceptable and unacceptable behavior. I was prepared with an experience chart (chart paper) and a black marking pen. I asked the children for class rules to remember. I recorded them in short sentences. The first was *WE DO NOT HIT. WE USE WORDS*. I elaborated on this saying that when someone was unkind or rough with us or hurt our feelings, we might get angry and tell them to stop or to "leave me alone," or we might say, "You are hurting my feelings," but we do not hit. We tell the teacher and we move away.

My efforts during the first weeks of school are to "shape" behavior in acceptable ways. So I give everyone a sticker on the first day. Thereafter, stickers become coveted rewards. It never fails to amaze me how children love stickers. So I buy the fanciest, most iridescent ones I can find and give them out every two or three days just before the class is dismissed, (This is advisable as they are quickly lost or fall off.) But the value of stickers is that they represent a reward for successful efforts to conform in the ways that the school emphasizes. The child can say, proudly, to Mommy or Daddy, "I got a sticker today." Helpful hint—If it has already disappeared, give the kid another. Stickers are examples of "positive reinforcements." Giving stickers pleases the children and increases the possibility that cooperation will continue and grow stronger over time. I gave Henry a sticker so that the pleasure connected with cooperation would be felt. Rewarding him was helping to shape his behavior. At the same time stories were being read and songs and poems were being learned about self-control, not hitting, and respecting others.

One morning, when the class was sitting on the rug, Henry kicked two children in fifteen minutes. On the way to the bathroom, Henry walked down the hallway, swinging a sweater, and making loud noises. Because one of our class rules was "We Walk Quietly in the Hallway," Henry was taken by the hand and stationed beside the teacher. When later that morning, he actually hit my educational assistant, his mother was called on her cell phone to discuss his behavior. Because he seemed out of control, I decided to keep him in at lunchtime (he said that he was going to kick Larry during lunch hour). When the class walked to the lunchroom, Henry got a tray but returned to the classroom with the teacher. This is an interesting situation. On one hand being alone with the teacher is pleasant for most children. After all, the child has the teacher's complete attention. I had a chance to talk quietly with a very difficult little boy. On the other hand, the situation must not become so pleasant that the child manufactures incidents that will cause him to be kept in. We ate lunch. I gave him time to look at picture books. Then I talked with Henry about how I had to protect the children, so I could not let him go into the yard and hit a child. I held his two hands in mine and said, "These hands are not for hitting. They are for writing and drawing and building with blocks. But they are not for hitting. Do you understand? What do the Rules say?"

I soon discovered that Henry's constant attacks had unusual roots. There were things about the family that I did not know. It was early in the school year and much is revealed in the classroom as time goes by. One day, I saw Henry do a "drop kick." It is a frightening high kick that aims for the person's head. I remember this action from my days of watching professional wrestling as a teenager. When I asked Henry about his television viewing, he admitted that he watched wrestling regularly and could do many of the "moves" because he was taking "karate" lessons. Anyone would be able to imagine the conversation that I had with Henry's parents at the end of the school day. He was terrorizing my class with strategies that he was learning from a professional. At the same time my understanding of "karate" was that it was a defensive strategy used when threatened with attack. Since Henry was using karate in a most aggressive way, I had to question the competency of instructors who did not teach the underlying philosophy of the sport, and I had to question Henry's need for such lessons. After all, no one was attacking him! He was acting like the Terminator! I asked his parents to consider discontinuing the lessons. Perhaps they could substitute swimming or music lessons.

But there seemed to be more to Henry's behavior than aggression learned while pursuing a sport. He punched girls as hard as boys. He hit the assistant teacher more than once. He never attacked me directly but once when I told him to go back to his seat, he said to me, "I'll smack you." He was constantly expressing a rage toward individuals and toward his teachers. Let's not forget his behavior toward his parents. Whenever his father was present, he was silent, his eyes wide, his body rigid. He sometimes answered his father, "Yes, sir!" His father was bigger, stronger, obviously a consumer of alcohol. I have no doubt that his father was physically capable of controlling him and abusing him. He was clearly afraid of his father but he never expressed feelings about his male parent. However, I did hear him say that he hated his mother. We are talking about a five-year-old child!

The family dynamic seemed important here. Because his father worked in the evening, he was available to bring his son to school. When I got on the cell phone to call Mom, in no time at all both Mom and Dad appeared. Dad would stand nose to nose with Henry and talk quietly but menacingly to the child. Interestingly, the moment his parents were gone, he reverted to negative behavior. When both parents sat in on lessons, Henry was quiet.

There were times when I wondered if his behavior wasn't "feral." In sociology, a feral child was one reared away from humans, purportedly by animals. Such a child was unsocialized and had not learned proper ways of behaving. The term is sometimes used to describe children who are reared in isolation and are so neglected that they do not develop as normal human beings. Could it be that this child was isolated in his bedroom and ignored for long periods? This would explain his corrosive anger.

Henry not only had parents but a younger brother of about eighteen months. His parents assured me that he loved his brother and enjoyed playing with him. An extremely important element in this family was that mother and father were separated. They were constantly seen together at school with baby brother but father no longer lived at home. Other class parents suggested that drugs and alcohol both had caused Henry's mother to ask him to leave. Now the separation of parents will cause the best adjusted child to become so distressed that classroom behavior changes. Was Henry's anger at everyone and everything a reaction to his parents' separation? Research shows that children who "act out" are often reacting when a beloved parent has been taken away or is no longer there to bond with and enjoy.

FROM BLACK CHILD CARE-

James P. Comer, M.D. and Alvin F. Poussaint M.D.

. . . Children who have been neglected, rejected or brutalized, in one way or another often show a brutality and harshness which is beyond the ordinary. Sometimes this is a sign that psychological problems exist which will require professional help. On the other hand, if teachers understand that there are reasons for this behavior and do not simply consider the child "bad," they can be very helpful . . . although you don't want to tolerate such behavior.

Youngsters who are cruel or rough usually have had difficult experiences with powerful adults. Their reaction is to try to control adults through provocative, negative, even threatening behavior—or to take their anger out on animals or children who don't fight as well as they do. They often are distrustful of adults and need evidence they can trust you. Such trust comes through your being fair and respectful to everyone in the classroom. This includes the teacher aide, parents and the custodian who comes in from time to time. A distrustful child will often provoke and test you to see if you are for real . . . whether you honestly care and are really concerned about him and others. If you make an effort to help the youngster but become provoked by his behavior, shout, and punish, your response will enable him to say, "See, I knew it all the time," even though he will probably not say so out loud.

If you lose control, it's not the end of the world. Gather your cool and say that you're sorry. But then calmly point out that there are certain things you expect in the classroom. You can also use a situation like this to help the youngster see what he does to you and other people to cause what he considers mistreatment to himself. Such incidents provide the opportunity for "verbal contracts"—you play fair with me and I'll play fair with you; you live by the reasonable rules of the classroom and I will be better able to be fair with you.

Because Henry's relationship with his father seemed so stilted and formal and not warm I want to offer some theories that could explain this ferocious young man. One relates very much to his mother. In *Black Rage* (1968) William Grier and Price Cobbs, both psychiatrists, discuss the role that a black woman must play in rearing sons in America. While the threat of lynching or physical harm from whites is less prevalent than it once was, black mothers are still mindful of their responsibility in helping their children adjust to the roles that they must play as adults. Because the care and rearing of the children falls to her, the black mother understands that the world is a dangerous place where her children will meet continuous obstacles. Race is an overwhelming obstacle. In an impoverished community like Henry's, the black child, especially the male child, is "beset by forces larger than his individual experience." The authors state flatly that "there are rules which regulate black lives far more than the lives of white[s]." As she shapes the character of her children, the black mother must "interpret" the society and its hidden messages to them.

> When black men recall their early life, consistent themes emerge. For example, the mother is generally perceived as having been sharply contradictory. She may have been permissive in some areas and punitive and rigid in others. There are remembrances of stimulation and gratification coexisting with memories of deprivation and rejection. There is always a feeling that the behavior of the mother was purposeful and deliberate ... The black man remembers that his mother underwent frequent and rapid shifts of mood. He remembers the cruelty. The mother who sang spirituals gently at church was capable of inflicting senseless pain at home. These themes of gratification and cruelty are consistent enough to suggest that they played a critical role in preparing the boy for adulthood. It would seem that the boy had to experience the polarities of ambivalence so that he could understand his later role in a white society.

Grier and Cobbs emphasize the socialization patterns that still exist within the black community. The mother must halt the kind of masculine assertiveness that spells danger in the world outside the home. The case of Amadou Diallo is a clear example of a situation where the mere perception of aggression is met with a hail of bullets by the police. (*The New York Times.* "Officers in Bronx Fire 41 shots, And an Unarmed Man is Killed," February 5, 1999.) However, an offshoot of the civil rights struggle in the United States is a competing need to be manly, to stand up for one's rights. The urban violence of the 1950s, 1960s, and 1970s in America presented a new model of behavior for young men. We must think of the black mother, who has put necessary restraints on her young child in the interests of self-preservation. She must then watch him join protests and demonstrations, fearful, yet feeling proud.

All of this has had an effect on my five-year-old student. He lives in an impoverished part of Harlem, subjected to the restraints placed on him by a reality-oriented mother, also exposed to the random violence, domestic violence, and lack of control of a hard-drinking father. Let us add to this mix, the constant exposure of television violence (from cops-and-robbers shows, but also from the bone-crushing mayhem of wrestling).

Grier and Cobbs suggest one additional ingredient that I think is all-important in explaining the rage of my kindergarten student. The authors are talking about the restlessness and tension that the black youngster feels at puberty. They note that he feels anger toward his father and is "alternately attracted to and repelled by his mother." I believe that Henry feels these things and something more. He is a very bright youngster, able to articulate his feelings and emotions. I think that even at five years, Henry, the child who "hangs out" with his father and his drinking buddies while his mother shops, has begun to realize something. He realizes that his father and the fathers of his friends are lacking something. "The authors are talking about an "historical legacy" that causes the adolescent to understand that "their schools are inferior, their neighborhoods are less attractive, and that their fathers and mothers make less money than their white counterparts." These latter facilities and financial arrangements have very little significance for a five-year-old child. However, I believe that at five years, Henry has had a similar realization. They *are* all lacking something—their families lack stability; there is constant conflict, and while there is affection there may not be much civility (much cursing, some hitting, not much reasoned discussion). Because Henry is beginning to read, he looks at picture books daily. We have a library full of books containing pictures of happy families. While in our class unit on "Families" we stress the variety of family units that exist (a large number of my pupils live with grandmothers; single-parent families are the norm in this community; there are even some same-gender couples with children). Nevertheless, the wide range of storybooks picture harmonious, cheerful family groups.

The institution of education exists in our society to prepare its children for productive participation as adults. While teachers have every right to accept and support the family groupings that exist, they must also present models of behavior that are accept-able in the larger society. The American ideal is the nuclear family of father, mother, and children. *Sesame Street*, situation comedies like *Everybody Loves Raymond*, *The Simpsons*, all show the ideal form even if some of its members are strange or comical or bizarre.

At the same time, coloring books, movies, storybooks also illus-trate the norm. They tell us what exists (i.e., single-parent group-ings) but they subtly suggest what *should exist*. A good example of this occurs whenever a teacher discusses the family structure. We ask the children, "Who's in your family?" We may use a flannel board and attach figures of mothers, fathers, grandmothers, broth-ers and sisters to it but inevitably, at story time we use *The Three Bears*—a classic, and delightful, but an illustration of the nuclear family at its uncomplicated best. Little Henry is constantly able to compare his often violence-torn family with the images that his teacher presents.

I am then suggesting several strands that come together to pro-duce the unmanageable children that we are seeing in our schools. It is regrettable but in the past parents used physical force to control their children. Children could be beaten by parents, and with the parent's permission, by teachers. Parents were mindful of their children's behavior in school and were anxious to support the school and its goals. However, parental controls have weakened. In today's society, corporal punishment is frowned upon. Children can be removed from a home and committed to foster care. Many par-ents have lost the autonomy that their parents and grandparents had. With single parents working, spending less time with their children, trying to manage a household, trying to have an adult social life, a lot of children are getting less socialization than ever. While Mom is balancing shopping, cooking, laundry, the kids may be watching television, playing video games for long periods. As they watch and absorb, on a subliminal level they are making comparisons. At the kindergarten stage, the teacher's view of things begins to challenge the mother's. In fact mothers frequently tell us about situations where the child refuses to accept the parent's view because the teacher has suggested something quite different.

Henry is angry about a lot of things. After much turmoil, his father has left the home. The family circle has been broken. His mother attempts to control him but has difficulty. The child tests her but feels insecure as she struggles with him. He is angry that the calm and orderly situations that he sees in books, on television and in the movies are not a part of his life. Because he is so young, because his mother has not embarked on the patient, careful training that middle class mothers emphasize—no hitting, using words to express his concerns, learning to delay gratification in relation to needs, learning to control impulses that might get him into trouble, all his angry feelings simmer inside. And because he lives in a community where he sees adults in physical confrontations and the police called to control behavior, it is not surprising that Henry's first impulse is to strike as those around him do. One additional thought . . . It is my impression, based on years of observing families, that some parents, on some level, enjoy their children's acting-out behavior. There is something that I see in their eyes or observe in their behavior as I complain about their children's aggression. Could it be that, on some level, they are saying . . . "Well . . . He's all boy!" It's cute until they get tired of being called to the school.

Another scenario comes to mind . . . This one represents the result of a young mother's rage. Until recently, Harlem, like many impoverished communities, had an exploding population of adolescent girls who were getting pregnant. These girls, dependents themselves, had been largely unprepared for motherhood. Together with their youth and lack of education, there existed some societal norms or rules that placed value on the need for marriage or the demand that the "baby's daddy" take responsibility. When he came forward to help support his child, payments might be sporadic, the result of his frequent unemployment, or possibly the fact that he was still in school or worse, that he drifts out of difficult situations and frequently on to a new relationship. The burden of child-rearing often falls on the young girl, her mother and the Administration for Children's Services. There is always an attempt to get the father involved but without economic resources his involvement is inconsistent, undependable, and infuriating. (If he has no money, "baby's daddy" will not be there on the child's birthday.) At a certain point, the young mother begins to realize that she will be a single parent. While caring for infants can be satisfying to young women who need affection and nurturance themselves, babies grow up. And they begin to look more and more like the scoundrel who deserted them. A thoughtful teacher in my school has often wondered if struggling young mothers don't begin to psychologically distance themselves from their male children feeling great ambivalence toward a young child who is a constant reminder of the man who has deserted her as she faces the difficulties of raising their child. She may feel towering rage at the careless, unsupportive individual who is not there in sickness or crisis, when bills do not get paid or the rent money is due. He is gone but not forgotten as she looks at his child before her. Mother enjoyed the infant but not the "answering-back" child. And her treatment of the child may cause him to feel a lack of the warmth and love that he needs.

Is this how a rage develops that is directed outward at his classmates, those more powerless than he?

EFFORTS TO CHANGE HENRY'S BEHAVIOR—DAILY CONTACT WITH THE MOTHER, FATHER, AND / OR CAREGIVER

At four and a half or five years someone has to bring the child to school. This gives me a chance to tell parents directly what is happening. Although some harried parents deposit their children in the schoolyard and rush away so as not to be late for work, (this is very dangerous because there is no adult supervision before a certain hour). And although some parents won't come in the schoolyard, pretty certain that the teacher will be there to pounce on them with bad news, Henry's mother and father came daily and . . . hopefully.

Henry listened to the parent-teacher exchange; there were often positive comments (i.e., his verbal contributions during class) but I never shrank from telling them about his bullying and aggression. They always listened, talked to him, then left. Yet *the value of daily reports*, of lack of progress, lay in the fact that they could not deny the problem or the fact that things were not getting better. Also, children would rush up to them to tell about their altercations with Henry. When parents see that their withdrawal of privileges, "time-outs," talks, and threats make no difference, they are more willing to sit down with me to find a solution to the problem of antisocial behavior.

CONTROLLING THE PHYSICAL ENVIRONMENT—ISOLATION, TIME-OUT, CRISIS INTERVENTION

Children like Henry who are physically aggressive must be isolated in order to protect others. They lack the ability to control their impulses so the teacher must create an environment where they can be comfortable and their peers safe. Such a child will be near me at all times. I almost never sit at my desk, but wherever I am, Henry is there also. In the meeting area, he will be beside me. He doesn't like it but his seat is not at a table. It is somewhat removed from the rest of the class. Whereas kindergarteners sit at tables to write or draw, during "Choice Time" or "free play" there are usually three or four children who sit in single seats, somewhat removed. We talked about this frequently during teacher-child conferences with constant restatement of the rules. Offenders joined the class for meeting time, but even then, if they did not use words but hit or pushed or kicked, they had to return to their seats.

We also had an area called our "time-out" corner. Children were sent to this area until they could regain control of themselves (if they were fighting, using unacceptable language). Occasionally a child would refuse to go for a "time-out" even though they only remained there for ten minutes and would be allowed to return to the group when calmer. "Time-outs" do not have to be for a long time. Separation from the group is painful for most children and they usually pull themselves together so that they can return.

Sometimes it would be necessary to call the *crisis intervention team*. One year, several of the school aides had a special assignment. If a teacher phoned, they were expected to come to the classroom, remove an out-of-control child to another room where he or she would be detained for perhaps one period. The aides had received training in coping with temper tantrums or other negative behaviors. Most children brought schoolwork to complete during this time but the emphasis was mainly on calming the child, while the teacher was given time to restore order in the classroom. At times, the crisis intervention team might need to call in the school social worker, psychologist, or counselor. These trained personnel are always on-site, engaged in testing, evaluating, and placing children appropriately, or conducting therapy sessions with parental approval. Children who have been removed from their classroom, for antisocial behavior, are generally already known to school caseworkers, so as therapeutic professionals they can be valuable in crisis situations.

PREVENTATIVE ACTIONS IN THE MORNING

There were mornings when it was clear that Henry was getting off to a bad start. Conflict in the family was evident. Henry was sulking and Mom and Dad didn't seem to be speaking to each other. This was a day when Henry was going to get a hug, first thing. But I also began to experiment with creating situations that would ease him into the school day painlessly. A very effective one was to allow Henry to remove himself from the group, to take a book and go to the library corner, or take a puzzle or game and work alone at a table. He might stretch out on the floor and work quietly or even take paper and write a story.

Although he was not with the group he seemed to know every-thing that was happening and would occasionally call out answers from the other side of the room. This strategy was a good one because Henry had a chance to regain his composure after a dif-ficult morning before school. I could see that his rage had been so close to the surface that he was ready to lash out at any available target. Given time to regroup and relax, Henry might be alone for a half hour but at some point he would return to the group, more ready to participate in a positive way. Of course I had to have a talk with several students who thought that they would "act out" so that they could have a special "playtime," too. I reminded them of other mornings when Henry had attacked them. They began to see the value of Henry's "alone-time."

REWARDS FOR POSITIVE EFFORTS

Stickers are helpful in shaping behavior. I like to show them to the class at the beginning of the day although they are not given out until dismissal time.

I like to encourage the class by stating certain rewards early in the day. During Morning Meeting I might tell Henry (with the class listening in) that if we have a pleasant day with coopera-tive behavior he will be line leader of the lunch line . . . and leader when we go upstairs to the art room, etc.

It is very meaningful to let parents know when Henry is improv-ing or at least making a real effort, so while the children are putting on their coats at dismissal time, I write a note detailing Henry's efforts. It is a good idea to have some cutouts available for this pur-pose. Using construction paper it is easy to cut out and color a big red apple or a flower to write on. Sometimes I ask the class to help me write the letter to Mom (i.e., Tommy Jones thanked Henry for helping him put the blocks away at cleanup time.)

Believe me, the children are delighted to say good things about their classmates.

It is important to change Henry's feelings toward his classmates.

I can think of two experience charts that might help. First we could create an experience chart called, "Things We like about Henry." I knew it would give this young man much pleasure. Eventually, we could create one called, "Henry's Friends in Kindergarten."

In April or May when they can express themselves as writers, I might encourage the class to write letters to Henry. If he is still aggressive, the children will get satisfaction from telling him how they feel. It will be a "wake-up call" for him when he sees it in writing.

Because I run a tight ship and follow a demanding schedule, it is only fair that I give my children special rewards also. One of these is that on Friday afternoons, we relax. We pop popcorn, or have those long pretzels, or grapes, and we watch movies. I have a whole collection of science films (i.e., about dinosaurs, the weather, animal stories) but I also have fairy tales, *Curious George, Madeline*, Bill Cosby films, and films based on library books.

The children are allowed to lie down on the rug, whisper, and in general "kick back," with the understanding that they have performed at a high level, did their very best, and I am proud of them. I let them choose from a catalog of films that they have seen, and who cares if they have seen *Madeline's Christmas* ten times. Just go with the flow!

HARSH MEASURES

I knew from the beginning that Henry was going to be with me for the whole year. When I requested that something be done about this child, the principal was unyielding and overwhelmed. We had many violent, difficult children. Our reading scores were low; our school was not in the upscale part of Harlem (called the "Gold Coast"). A good indicator of our low-income status was the fact that all our children were eligible for free lunch. Because of low reading scores, we were not a magnet school with special programs and middle-class parents orchestrating their children's academic progress. When I was in a bad mood, I would call our school "a dumping ground." Because our enrollment was low, we accepted any child who came, including kids who had been expelled from other schools. Because we did not have a good reputation, we could not get or hold topflight teachers. When I asked the principal to move Henry to another class, she asked me where that might be. She was really saying that I was a strong teacher and could handle him. All her other kindergarten teachers could not. His mother would not allow him to be tested. Frequently parents reject testing, fearing a special education placement. So he would remain with me.

My hair was beginning to fall out from stress, so I figured that it was time for harsh measures. By this I mean "tough love," kindergarten style. I had a plan. In November, I take my class to the American Museum of Natural History and the planetarium. Now a class trip is harrowing because the teacher cannot relax until all twenty-plus children are back in school safe and sound. I must reserve a school bus, arrange for lunches to be carried with us, select some capable parents to accompany us, get signed permission slips for each child, notify the office that we are going, and on the day of the trip, sign the class out officially, leave my roll book with the day's attendance in the office after toileting the whole class so we would not have any accidents on the bus or in the museum. We had practiced walking with a partner, talked about noise levels, etiquette on the bus, and periodic checks where I count heads.

I was well aware that I could not take Henry. I could not risk fighting in the museum or during the "sky show." Henry was a child lacking in self-control. In unfamiliar surroundings such a child was a walking time bomb. Also, I have many responsibilities on a trip day. It is my job to sign the class in at the museum and pay for the admission of children, parents, and my assistant, get ID tags for each of us, guide us up on several elevators and walk the class through the dinosaur exhibits.

I asked Henry's mother if one of his parents could come on the trip. She said it was not possible. I explained that I could not be responsible for the whole class *and* Henry. Safety was my primary concern. I found it strange that Henry didn't believe me. He kept saying, "I'm going." In the days before the trip, his behavior was totally unacceptable then on the day before the trip, at dismissal, his mother whispered in his ear and he came over to tell me that he would behave on the trip. I told his mother that she could either keep him at home or I could arrange for him to be in another class for the day.

AND HE DID NOT GO. It was important for Henry and his mother to realize that I could be consistent, that I meant what I said. His propensity to hit or push made him a problem (that I did not need). However, I let him know that if he learned to use words to express his desires and feelings, he would be able to go on the next trip. If he continued to use his hands to hurt others, I would not take him to The National Museum of the American Indian or the zoo. Henry was sulky and angry and resentful. Now was the time for choices and for him to take control in a meaningful way. Henry had many "shaping" influences now—glowing letters to his mom when he was cooperative, ability to separate himself from the group when he needed to control himself, conferences with the teacher when we could evaluate his progress, feedback from his classmates as they evaluated his behavior, stickers, and other positive reinforcements when he was showing effort, and now a clear signal about what he would forfeit if he did not improve (inability to take class trips).

Prior exclusion from the first class trip made Henry determined to go on the next one. A situation actually occurred in which he had begun a fight, I threatened him, "Stop now or you won't go . . ." He dropped his hands, saying, "I want to go on the trip." This was a major milestone!

AN IMPORTANT STEP FORWARD—THERAPEUTIC HELP

However, I would not brag and feel triumphant. We, at the school, were making a concerted effort to help Henry mature but his mother's efforts were extremely important. She began to cooperate with a social service agency to get counseling for her son. Possibly she began to wonder about the frequency of his aggression even though she and her husband were constantly talking to him and verbalizing their disapproval. Possibly she began to think about his school career. Henry was in kindergarten. If he did not learn to control his impulses now, things were going to get worse. She agreed to take him to an outpatient unit of a local hospital. The family was in crisis and professional help would give her the support that she needed in dealing with her husband and her son. Things began to get better as Henry began to receive attention and services from the school and social service personnel at the hospital. This courageous mother understood that help from cooperating individuals and agencies would effect a change.

The socialization of aggressive children like Henry frequently depends on the cooperation of the teacher and the guidance department within the school. In our school we have a team on-site (guidance counselor, social worker, psychologist and a person trained to test and evaluate children). If parents are not prepared to seek help from an outside agency, they can look to the school for professional help for their child. In close cooperation with the teacher, parents can expect and receive counseling for their children where classroom behavior is unacceptable but also in cases of bereavement, divorce, separation or other crisis situations. Small group or individual sessions can be scheduled in a routine way and a social service person will pick up the child and return him/her to the classroom after a session.

It would be wrong to suggest that Henry became a model student. However, I can say that when spring came he was less threatening, the children were less frightened and I was less tired at the end of the day.

9

Critical Thinking and Creative Thinking

THINKING CRITICALLY

If one of the primary goals of education is the development of mature citizens capable of functioning effectively in American society, then a crucial skill to be learned is the habit of critical thinking. When reading the papers, voting for governmental leaders, choosing our children's schools, shopping for the best insurance policy, we must make important decisions that have far-reaching results. On the other hand, even small children are confronted with the need to think critically and they also make decisions continually. When confronted with a shelf of learning materials and games, the kindergartener must choose something with which to occupy him- or herself. This decision may be based on interest, curiosity, or the colorful packaging of a box. However, the same child must make more serious decisions—which children to avoid in the playground, which foods to choose during lunchtime, remembering Mommy's concerns about getting fat, or after discussion on the mat, what drawing to make that best follows the teacher's directions about the "animal of the week."

As educators scramble to improve the quality of education and to raise the achievement scores of disadvantaged schoolchildren, they understand the need to encourage the development of higher levels of decision-making in all students. It is clearly understood that in order to change student performance in all areas of the curriculum, children must develop the skill of critical thinking so that they can greatly improve the quality of their intellectual responses. There are many ways to think about the classroom activities that would encourage critical thinking and lead to higher-level academic performance. A favorite tool that I have used in developing lessons is the influential classification scheme known as Bloom's Taxonomy (New York, 1956).

Benjamin Bloom has created classifications or criteria that could be used by educators and psychologists in test construction, in research, and curriculum planning. The significant thing about them is that they can be used at any level of instruction (from kindergarten to graduate school). They are valuable in evaluating student responses based on the level of complexity shown. Bloom's Taxonomy is a hierarchical model.

This means that the levels of the model become increasingly complex, and the author and his associates accept the notion that the higher levels cannot be reached without an understanding of all the levels below. There are six levels. They range from knowledge to comprehension, application, analysis, synthesis, and evaluation. Even though this book is aimed at kindergarteners and the levels of the Taxonomy are abstract and very sophisticated, the authors believe that all children, with time, attention, and solid teaching experiences are capable of functioning on the higher levels of the Taxonomy and improving the quality of their intellectual responses.

Levels of the Taxonomy

- *Knowledge*—Information that has been learned. The student remembers facts, classifications, trends, abstractions, theories, principles. These have been memorized and are a part of the student's knowledge base. To Bloom, knowledge is "rote memory." A lively way to illustrate these levels is to discuss a "dinosaur curriculum." *Accordingly, "knowledge" could be illustrated by answering the question, "What are the characteristics of ten dinosaurs?"*

- *Comprehension*—On this level, the individual can translate knowledge (paraphrase it, using one's own words), interpret knowledge (explain or summarize it), extrapolate knowledge (to extend it, to go beyond it), to predict based on facts known. *Comprehension might be illustrated by asking "Why are they dinosaurs, not lizards?"*

- *Application*—Here applying knowledge is expected. If one learns abstractions or rules of procedure, then one is expected to be able to apply them to a problem or situation. The basic idea is to be able to apply knowledge learned to a different circumstance. *Application would lead to the construction of a brontosaurus.*

- *Analysis*—In order to understand, it is necessary to break a structure into its component parts and then to see the relationship of the parts. At this level, analysis of elements of the structure (the parts), analysis of relationships, and analysis of organizational principles must be undertaken. *An analysis might focus on the question, "What biological family do dinosaurs belong to?"*

- *Synthesis*—If analysis involves "taking apart," then synthesis involves "putting together." Elements are combined or rearranged to create something that was not there before. *A synthesis of information learned might answer the question, "Did dinosaurs become birds?"*

- *Evaluation*—The highest level, illustrating the highest cognitive skill is *evaluation*. At this level one has the ability to make judgments about the value of something. If asked, "Is this painting beautiful?" a response would be based on the following: External evidence helping one to judge might be to compare the painting with other paintings agreed to be of high quality, judging based on standards accepted in a particular field or evaluating an idea by referring to a theory. Judgments made using internal evidence must be related to logical accuracy or consistency. *In order to deal with the value of the scientific theories that exist, it would be necessary to evaluate the question, "Was it inevitable that dinosaurs would become extinct?"* The dinosaur analogies were suggested in a seminar on education at Columbia University during 1991 (Project Synergy Fellows).

Bloom's Taxonomy is a well-known and much used instrument in American schools and colleges. It has long been used in the area of "gifted education." The assumption, of many of those who want to use the Taxonomy as a teaching tool, is that it is possible to develop learning activities that encourage the types of thinking that Bloom describes, and in time, cognitive processes will be improved. Teachers of the gifted believe that such children have the capacity to think at high levels of complexity and have given much attention to activities that encourage analysis, synthesis, and evaluation. C. June Maker in her survey of the field, *Teaching Models in Education of the Gifted* (1995) suggests caution in the application of such assumptions. She notes that while it is true that gifted children do usually possess a "wide range of information," the need for emphasis on "knowledge" and "comprehension" is overlooked and these levels are neglected. "In attempting to concentrate on the higher levels, educators often forget to check children's knowledge and understanding of the concepts found at lower levels. A related assumption is that gifted children *should* spend more time at higher levels because this type of thinking is more challenging for them.

Maker's observations about neglect of the lower levels of the Taxonomy have resonance for two reasons. In an earlier discussion, I emphasized the value of *memorization* during my early years. My ability to memorize and perform "The Night before Christmas" at the age of seven, gave me strengths and abilities and increased the "cultural capital" that I brought to school (pp. 2–3). I believe that lack of emphasis on the knowledge level is unfair to the young learner. Knowledge provides a base, a storehouse for the material that becomes more sophisticated and subtle as it is shaped conceptually by experience and more learning.

While I consider this a cornerstone of my pedagogical practice, Maker notes that scholars disagree with Bloom about the role that knowledge plays. There is some question about the degree to which the levels of the Taxonomy depend on each other. Other researchers have questioned the ordering of the levels of the Taxonomy. Some research shows that *evaluation* does not illustrate the highest level of cognitive behavior and indeed may not have been placed at the right level in the Taxonomy (Stoker and Kropp, 1964). There are a number of questions yet to be answered about the *validity* of the Taxonomy. Maker points to some of these. For example, are the levels really arranged from simple to complex? And does each higher level of the Taxonomy depend on the levels below it? Although the Taxonomy is widely used, Maker questions the lack of research showing its "effectiveness" with children, particularly the gifted. Also "the review of research has not uncovered evidence that the use of the [taxonomy would] have the hypothesized effect of improving higher levels of thinking. Ultimately, Maker finds that the Taxonomy has value as it shows the "relative emphasis" on higher and lower thinking processes in gifted programs but further research would make it "more defensible" in curriculum development.

INDICATIONS OF GIFTEDNESS PERCEIVED IN MINORITY CHILDREN

While I believe that these traits are found in most gifted children I am stressing that these are behaviors that I observed in my Harlem kindergarten. I remember creating this list in the summer after the academic year was over.

1. Gifted children have the ability to figure things out. I brought a new toy to class called Jacob's Ladder. It was a series of connected wooden blocks, which, because of cotton bands, clatter up and down like magic. Because I am challenged by anything that is remotely mechanical, I could not figure out how to make it go. Isaiah G. did. This five-year-old child showed me that the movement of the blocks was caused by the action of the wrist.

2. Bright children usually have highly developed memories and increase their vocabularies easily. If I teach a new word (such as enormous), the next day they remember the word and can verbalize it again. Yvonne is particularly good at this. They are able to remember the main idea of a previous lesson and discuss it. They have good memories plus they understand the basic concepts.

3. Certain children will figure out new ways to use materials or will take open-ended materials and create something new. Karim made a helicopter with a blade that turned. He created a series of toys that spun around because he discovered that if you put a dowel through a rectangular piece with a hole that was slightly bigger, you could spin the rectangular piece.

4. Bright children can see relationships. They do not know what a syllogism is but can work out the details or illustrate a syllogism.

5. ESL children can translate from their native language to English for the teacher.

The following diagrams and charts illustrate some of the ways my classes of kindergarteners have responded to the Taxonomy and engaged in critical thinking.

THE PILGRIMS

They made houses out of wood.   The Pilgrims grew corn.

(Anthony)

Squanto helped them catch fish and wild turkeys and deer
(Anthony, Malcolm, Avery)

They had Thanksgiving
to give thanks.

         The King wouldn't let them
         go to their own church.

           (Aaron)

Some of them died.   They went on the

(Robert)   Mayflower.

           (Dana)

The above observations were part of a Venn diagram made to remember what we had learned about Thanksgiving and the story of the Pilgrims. The results are paraphrases of the Pilgrims' story. This is an example of the children's use of their own words to explain Thanksgiving. They are operating at the level of *COMPREHENSION*.

In my kindergarten, we always discussed the *seasons of the year*. This curriculum was valuable as it encouraged learning about the natural world and sparked all kinds of science projects. The following experience chart shows the knowledge that the children gained and their ability to think at the level of *APPLICATION*. They are using knowledge learned and applying it to a problem posed by the teacher:

PROBLEM—SUPPOSE THERE WAS NO SPRING? (APPLICATION)

BRITTNEY: Winter would stay forever.

RAY SEAN: The flowers wouldn't grow. The seeds wouldn't grow without the sun and rain.

TREVOR: You couldn't ride your bike.

ANTHONY: Snow would come down.

DANIEL: You couldn't play outside.

NIJA: You would wear a coat.

NAKEEM: No grass would grow.

SOLOMON: You could skate on the ice.

DAVID: There wouldn't be food.

EBONY: The apple blossoms wouldn't grow.

TAHIRAH: The bears would stay in their caves.

In encouraging critical thinking skills in my kindergarteners, I was most often interested in the level of *ANALYSIS*. I felt that the ability to make comparisons, to figure out what was the same and what was different called forth a kind of critical analysis that I prized in very young children. These are the same skills that a college student must use on an essay exam, so I devoted much attention to them.

The task is to examine TIGERS and BIRDS. The children were asked to compare them and decide what characteristics they shared and what characteristics they had that were different. I did not attach the children's names to their answers because I was concentrating on the concepts, same and different. Below I have reproduced an experience chart of their responses.

Their use of ANALYSIS is clear:

TIGERS AND BIRDS—WHAT IS THE SAME? WHAT IS DIFFERENT?

What is the same?

1. Both have warm blood.
2. Both live in the jungle.

3. Both need air.
4. Both drink water.
5. Both sleep.
6. Both have heads.
7. Both have eyes.
8. Some birds eat meat (i.e., eagles). Tigers eat meat.
9. Both have feet.

What is different?

1. Birds fly. Tigers run.
2. Birds are in trees. Tigers are on the ground.
3. Tigers have stripes. Tigers have fur. Birds have feathers.
4. Tiger babies are born alive. Bird babies come from eggs.
5. Tigers have ears. Birds don't.
6. Tigers have four legs.
7. Birds have two legs.

I am sorry to say that I made no attempt to explore the levels of synthesis and evaluation. I was elated that they had the ability to analyze events. I don't think that Bloom was thinking about kindergarteners when he conceptualized the Taxonomy. However I submit the following experience chart to suggest that perhaps I was wrong.

Books by Dr. Seuss

1. They rhyme. (Malik)
2. They are fun. (Jarett)
3. Some [characters] are bad and some are good. (Treasure)
4. They have "pretend" people. (Tori)
5. Some are funny and some are sad. The Grinch makes me feel disgusted. (Michael)
6. The pictures are fantastic. (Jarett)
7. They are like cartoons. (Treasure)

There were many ways to encourage critical thinking in my kindergarten. Because the children showed so much interest in these activities, it was easy to build them into my curriculum. We always devoted a big block of time to *Critical Thinking* every Wednesday. When the children were excited about a subject, their discussion continued for long periods. Besides the Taxonomy, I used other strategies that were productive.

At a workshop organized by the district office, I received some training in developing curriculum specifically for gifted children. I decided that I wanted to use the workshop materials with the whole class because they were diverse enough to challenge *all* the children regardless of skill level, and I wanted to see *all* the children exposed to exciting experiences. However, it was also important to give special projects to my brightest children because it is not wise to hold them back while the rest are catching up. I frequently prepared work for them to do alone or in small groups so they could follow other lines of inquiry. My ablest youngsters learned to read and write more quickly than their peers so they were able to do writing assignments and research on their own. One of the resources that I used with the whole class was a staff development manual called *It's Time for Talents*. (1987) This manual was developed by the Division of Curriculum and Instruction for use in the Talents Unlimited Program, a training program for teachers initiated within the New York City public schools. This program recognized the variety of cognitive abilities that children exhibit, and it was hoped, that through systematic training, one could nurture these cognitive abilities or "talents" and develop critical thinking skills throughout the curriculum. The manual emphasizes a "hierarchy of skills." These are productive thinking, communication, forecasting, decision-making, and planning.

There are many differences between *Bloom's Taxonomy* and the hierarchy of skills or "talents" found in the staff development manual, *It's Time for Talents*. Bloom focuses on a quantity of information that can be manipulated in several ways. For example, a student could illustrate the classification *comprehension* of information, in the

Taxonomy, by these tasks—paraphrasing, interpreting, or extrapolating information. In *It's Time for Talents*, the skill of productive thinking is *less* the manipulation of information but *more* the generation of information. Productive thinking is really "divergent thinking." The student who exhibits productive thinking is less concerned with complexity of thought or quality of output and rather more concerned with "what is different" or "coming up with a lot of new stuff." Here the productive thinking talent is much like E. P. Torrance's factors of fluency, flexibility, originality, and elaboration (1965, 1979) where the child is asked to generate many "varied" and "unusual" responses. Indeed the strategy of generating ideas based on imagination, originality and quantity is typical of Torrance, an influential researcher in the field of creativity, who devised and tested measures called *The Torrance Tests of Creative Thinking.* (1962, 1972)

I am a kindergarten teacher interested in encouraging critical thinking skills in my children and Bloom's Taxonomy became an important tool for me to use. However, I have another responsibility also. It is imperative to develop learners with imagination and the ability to generate new ideas, new approaches, new systems. In the world that these children will grow up in, there will be many new technologies that we cannot even imagine at this time. Preparing children to live in a world that is as yet unimagined can only be possible if today's teachers can give them the gift of *creativity*. And it is possible to teach them to think expansively, to think "outside the box." This is where "knowledge" and "creativity" intersect. Young people stuffed with facts and information, exposed to all kinds of experiences, trained to think "expansively," will be unafraid to experiment and to seek new truths. Bloom's hierarchy offers the arsenal of knowledge, the basic facts or information to draw upon, the ability to play with ideas and interpret them or extrapolate them. If the learner can apply them to something new, can compare them with other experiences or ideas by analyzing them, the learner is moving toward synthesis, the construction of something creatively new. Bloom offers opportunities for both critical thinking of qualitative excellence as well as opportunities for creative expression.

I think the Taxonomy is more challenging intellectually than the theoretical underpinnings of *Time for Talents*. However the latter is a true gold mine of ideas for curriculum planning. It is a book, chock full of activities, conversations, experience chart lessons for every occasion. Because it encourages a freewheeling generation of ideas (fluency) it offers activities that call forth critical faculties as well as creative responses. Happily, I can find many overlapping concepts that illuminate these too. *Talents* is a treasure trove of lesson plans for kindergarten, mixed kindergarten and first grade classes, and first grade classes. The areas covered are communication arts, mathematics, social studies, science and arts.

To illustrate how this fabulous resource enriched my kindergarteners, I used a lesson called "The Cage Is Open." In the simplest terms, my children were able to respond to Bloom's level of "Application," giving answers that showed logical thought as well as varied and unusual solutions to the problem.

If all the cages at the zoo were opened, the following would result:

ROLANDA: All the animals would go out.

CARLOS: The tigers and the elephants would run out. The tigers would scratch you.

MAE: The monkeys would go up in the trees.

GLENN: The animals would run to another zoo to find new cages.

LORELLA: If they don't find a safe place, they would go back to their own cages.

KENNY: The cars might run over the turtles and frogs.

CHINA: The tigers and lions would eat you.

KELLEY: The zebras would find a new place to sleep.

BRITTNEY: The snakes would bite you.

While it is predictable that some children would focus on the mayhem that would result, notice that other children have more thoughtful responses. For example, one child suggests the animals would run to another zoo to find new cages; another child cautions that if the animals don't find new habitation that is safe, they will return to an environment that they are familiar with. Realistically, the monkeys would climb trees where they would be safe and one child shows concern for the smaller animals that might be run over by cars. The children imply that while we are not safe if all the cages are opened at the zoo, the animals themselves are not safe either. Notice that no one suggests that if the cages are opened some animals might remain in their cages. We have made trips to zoos where the animals are not in cages; the class shows awareness that cages are not good places for animals.

I believe that frequent classroom discussions have created critical awareness that is reflected or implied in their comments. This is what we are aiming for, children, who from an early age learn to reflect about all manner of things.

Another lesson where critical thinking was demonstrated used an experience chart and recorded responses dealing with *probabilities*. The children were asked to distinguish among three possibilities: What will happen? What might happen? What will never happen? The answers showed serious thought.

What will happen?

1. TIANA: A new tooth.
2. CELIA: You will grow.
3. CHINA: Going to a museum.
4. DWAYNE: Daylight will come.

What might happen? . . . (maybe)

1. GLORY: I'll have hamburger for lunch.
2. ZENA: I'll go to first grade.
3. DESTINY: Mom will buy you sneakers.
4. LUZ: We'll have an assembly.

What will never happen?

1. KENYA: Green rain.
2. BRIANA: Having a pony.
3. FRANCISCO: I'll shrink.

In our discussions, I sometimes ask them to think about an *abstraction*.

Being a friend

JERROD: Take a friend to the mall.

DESTINY: Push your friend on a swing.

MELVIN: Play basketball.

NAIROBI: Buy ice cream for them.

KENNY: Play racing cars.

ROSALEE: Play tag with them.

SARA: Go to the movies with them.

ERNESTO: Play Test Drive.

JORGE: Skate with them.

SHANEKA: Go to the beach.

DAVID: Ride bikes with them.

JANAE: Play with blocks and puppies.

JEM: Play Barbie dolls with them.

Just as I would like a class of thoughtful, inquiring youngsters, I would also like a class of clever, imaginative, playful, creative youngsters. In order to produce such children I believe that *reading and writing must be taught together*. Having visited a number of low-performing schools, I am well aware that while reading is stressed in all places, writing is handled differently. This may be because some teachers see writing as extraordinarily difficult, for themselves as well as for their pupils. For adults, the only way to improve as a writer is to write—letters, journals, term papers, essays, short stories . . . A writing course in graduate school is a good investment for any teacher who has cold sweats anytime a report must be sent to a guidance counselor or to the principal. With kindergarteners, who routinely begin writing skills as part of the curriculum during the year, it is easier than you think! I begin writing lessons as soon as the children have a few phonic sounds under their belts. If you will remember I said earlier that I teach them the sight word "like" in September. We use it continually. If the children bring in the cereal boxes they have just eaten out of at breakfast in the cafeteria, we write "I like Cheerios." Note that as children learn words, it is easy to teach them to leave spaces between them. Just tell them to put their finger next to the word and begin the new word on the other side of their finger. The important thing is to get them to write about things that they like . . . toys, Mommy, Daddy, books, the park, Saturday, holidays . . . or things that they do not like. You don't have to make suggestions. They will tell you immediately and will concentrate on writing with ferocity. As they ask for help with spelling, sounding out the letters for them as they write, works well, but this is a good opportunity to add words to the Word Wall. When we create an experience chart as a class, "I do not like" things come pouring out. Because my children love to use pointers and read experience charts to each other during Choice Time, they quickly learn about spacing and periods. With periods, I merely say that I put a period where my voice stops. Have a child read a sentence out loud. Where they finish a thought and their voice stops, insert a period. An easy sentence is "I do not like bedtime." Have the child (or the class) copy it. You will find that they tackle such sentences with enthusiasm. I remember one session when a student wrote, "I do not like Ms. Jones." The subject of the sentence was my student teacher. Oh well! Once they learn to write, they continually express their feelings and that is a good thing. Must find out what Ms. Jones has done! My students also use experience charts to develop their writing skills by copying. They are particularly eager to copy a sentence that they have contributed, and they proudly take the work home to show family members.

SIMILES

I want my children to be proficient writers. More than that, I want them to be interesting writers. Actually, I want them to be brilliant writers. I read them lively, colorful, imaginative books all the time. I like to enchant them. Because I have difficulty with dull books (in hot weather, I have been known to fall asleep when reading a boring story during story time), I have thought a good deal about producing brilliant writers. If we start in September, by the month of February, a number of them will be writing independently. But I want art. If they are exposed to good writing, stories that capture their imaginations, they will be more attuned to the possibilities of literature. I can also aid their development by giving them the tools that good adult writers have. One of my favorites is the *simile*. Its value in writing is to describe things by likening them to something else. For twenty years I have been taking chart paper and writing something like this . . . I like red things . . . as red as . . . Let's think of some red things. This is not wildly original. Probably only obvious! *It's Time for Talents* makes "Red! Red! Red!" the first lesson for kindergarteners in their communication arts chapter. In the classroom, the teacher introduces the lesson by pointing to a child wearing something red. The teacher explains that she is interested in things that are always red. Then she asks the class to think of "many, varied and unusual things that are always red." I like to say, "Think of red things . . . as red as . . ." I would then write down their responses. It is helpful to remind them that (as . . . as) sentences make their writing more exciting and grown-up. During creative writing periods, as I read their contributions, I implant the idea of similes by suggesting a comparison. If the child says, "I like to go fast on my bike," I say, "How fast? As fast as . . ." When the student comes up with a comparison I encourage him or her to write it down. Later on when the student reads a story during our Conference Time, I will point out and praise the use of a vivid comparison that gives the writing an imaginative sparkle or a zing, like a writer of a storybook. Often I can make a deal with another teacher so that a child who attempts these literary flourishes is permitted to go to a nearby class and read his or her creative work to another appreciative audience.

SIMILES ENCOURAGE IMAGINATION

Here are some examples.

I like soft things . . . as soft as . . .

    AMANDA: hair

    KAREEM: a rose

    TARIK: a teddy bear

    SHANIYA: a feather

    MIKA: a cushion

    NOELY: Play-Doh

    NEHENDRA: a dog's fur

    NYAISA: a shirt

    BYRON: a cloud

    ROSIE: a cat's fur

I like round things . . . as round as . . .

    JASMINE: circles

    COURTNEY: a ball, a yo-yo

    SAQUAN: a pumpkin, a pizza

    TAHIRAH: the bottom of a pole

    SONNELYS: a balloon, the letter O

    LUIS: a face, a cake, a doughnut

    NIJA: a lock

While I complimented all the children on their contributions I did ask the group about which answer was the most varied and unusual. I would help them to understand that Tahirah's answer was a surprise, because I never would have thought of it. It was an unusual answer, what we call thinking "outside the box," I challenged them to always think of varied and unusual answers . . . those answers that would surprise us and delight us.

WRITING AS A MEANS OF EXPRESSION

If creativity can be defined as creating products that are original and have not been copied, that express personal feelings and reveal the inner workings of the mind, I have a terrific example. This is a first-grade story because I followed my class from kindergarten to first grade at the request of my principal.

I was happy to comply because the kindergarten year had been a delight. There were a number of pupils who had learned to read and write and had begun to act in literate ways. Teaching them had been a joy. There were some negative factors though. We had to move from the ground floor to the second floor. Lest you think that my classroom years were all sunlight and roses, our new room was so mouse-ridden, that when we planted seeds to grow plants for Mother's Day, not one sprout came up because the mice had eaten every single seed. But this story is about children writing well enough to communicate thoughts and express feelings. One afternoon I found a paper on the floor. It was smudged and dirty and when I read it I was surprised. I have reproduced it so that you can read it, but there is a backstory that clearly shows the anguish and pain of a six-year-old. It said:

Tony, you is my only brother

I know Adream lik you

I know Adream is your girlfriend.

I like her to Tony.

Girls like Tony. No girls like me.

While I was touched by the pain that this child was expressing I was overwhelmed with pride that he was expressing himself in a literary way. Perhaps this paper had been discarded after he had made a clean copy. Never mind! He was thinking that writing was a good way to express himself and tell his friend Tony how he felt. There is more to the story because the charming Miss Adream read the letter (Tony must have shown it to her). She sent back a crushing reply.

Hat you (hate)

I love Tony

I dot (don't) lik you.

I hat you Rayman (Raymond).

* * *

Dear Courtney I ms you wen you went down south.

We lrnd letr X.

I had a brthday. Ray Sean

* * *

My Story by Alex

When I wokn up I hearbd a soune

It was coming from the kitchen It was

the water. I love you.

Several things became clear as I read the little stories that my children wrote. First of all, they were able to express themselves because they had phonics internalized (they could "sound out" words that they did not know how to spell. Words like "brthday," "letr" "hat" (for hate), "lik," are all intelligible, and they seem to have learned some difficult words like "when," "you," "kitchen" from the Word Wall. They had frequent chances to write and seemed to be developing working vocabularies. Because Spelling Bees were a regular Friday activity, there was much interest and pleasure in spelling correctly. By June they were much improved. The following experience chart shows how the children developed a feeling for elegant expression and poetic phrases and similes.

MY MOMMY

MICHAEL: My Mommy is as beautiful as the stars.

CORAIMA: She has designs on her pants.

SHAQUANNA: And diamonds on her shirts.

SEAN, TORI: She has sparkling rings and sparkling eyes.

MICHAEL: She helped me win a prize at Coney Island.

TORI, JANELLE: She gives me juice and peaches.

SHAQUANNA: I give her roses.

HASIM: I give her love; she gives me soft pillows.

PHILLIP: She lets me sleep with the night-light on.

TORI, MICHAEL: She reads me fairy tales about knights and dragons.

MICHAEL, SHAQUANNA: I feel happy when she kisses me because I know she loves me.

10

Principals I Have Known

I HAVE OFTEN WONDERED what makes a person want to be a principal. Time and cynicism have given me some answers. Apparently, it rarely has anything to do with leadership, altruism, or education. When I think back on the nine principals under whom I have served, it seems obvious that some sought career advancement, others more money and the rewards that come as families grow and niftier vacations beckon. But knowledge about their personalities, inner motivations and social environments suggest subtler blandishments, other needs that might be hidden from all but a few.

My first elementary school principal, Harold Sklar, embodied a kind of ideal. He was part of that group of educators who remembered or whose parents remembered "the Great Depression." Education offered a secure job, respectability, and a middle-class lifestyle. He was a kind, tweedy gentleman who looked a lot like Leonard Bernstein. His school, P.S. 68, a rambling, long building in Harlem, had a wing that dated back to the first decade of the twentieth century. Like my first school in Brooklyn, P.S. 54, this wing had sliding walls on tracks, so that the whole school could have assembly together. In 1961, Mr. Sklar's faculty seemed huge to me: twenty-five men and about twenty-five women. There were equal numbers of black and white teachers, but no educational assistants or paraprofessionals working in the classrooms. Generally fifth and sixth grade teachers were males. Except for one or two glaring exceptions, all of the teachers seemed able to control their classes and although a historic social ferment was beginning in the 1960s (the decentralization wars), the school was a friendly, orderly place.

I first visited the school to do an assembly program as a playground director, supervising a nursery school program near Stuyvesant Town in Manhattan. Because I was employed by the Department of Parks, I had the good fortune to become storyteller at the Hans Christian Andersen Memorial statue in Central Park, so it had become easy for me to enthrall a large audience. I did a few finger plays and then decided to tell a few "tall tales" about Paul Bunyan and his blue ox, Babe. The kids listened quietly and were wonderfully responsive at the end. Mr. Sklar let me know that I could come back whenever I wanted to. Sometime later, when I was actually teaching in an infamous junior high school (also in Harlem), a bomb threat was called in. The caller said that a bomb had been placed in the teacher's room. During my lunch hour, I ran around to Mr. Sklar's school. He hired me on the spot. I began teaching kindergarten that fall. My classroom, a huge room which accommodated half-day classes of fifty children in the morning and fifty children in the afternoon, was opposite the principal's office. The principal popped in occasionally and was kindness itself.

What was it like to teach fifty kids at one time? Not difficult. At that time, kindergarten was a preparatory situation.

Our chief mission was to get the children ready for the rigors of first grade where academic instruction would begin. They had to learn to follow directions, to learn socialization skills like lining up, to develop a repertoire of songs and games; to learn to hold a pencil, cut with scissors, and tying one's shoes was a major concern.

Velcro did not exist and fifty little ones trailing untied shoelaces was not to be tolerated. The morning teacher, Ms. Ball (known by the children as Mrs. Balls), provided instruction while I toileted children. In the afternoon I did the teaching. We suffered through a "snack time" where the children paid for milk and cookies, which we had to order, distribute, and for which we had to keep records. Note that when I was toileting, Ms. Ball was alone with fifty children just as I was alone in the afternoon. I now believe that the major sources or learning were music time (at that time all kindergarten teachers were supposed to be able to play the piano), story time and the *Weekly Reader* with its science and nature sections.

I soon found that some faculty members considered Mr. Sklar "too easy." They felt that he tried to please everybody. While he was disparaged by some, he was adored by the rest. To me, he was the nurturing male, a father figure after I had left my parental home. I now believe that all good principals, whether male or female, must have this nurturing skill. A school, contrary to the bureaucratic model of large organizations like the Board of Education, cannot be an impersonal, rationally regulated place. A corporate employee does not need to *enjoy* the workplace. Such a person needs to be competent, expects to be treated fairly, and hopes for rapid advancement. However a school is very different. A school must help to shape nascent personalities, provide a safe, secure and friendly environment where young children can internalize intellectual and social skills that will prepare them for adulthood, both vocationally and as citizens. If young children are distressed by brutal treatment on the part of teachers or other students, if they must exist in an unsafe environment (i.e., drug dealing in the school yard or drive-by shootings near the school) they will not thrive.

So as a classroom teacher, responsible for the intellectual development of a new generation of Americans, I have a special view of principals. They are "enablers." They are there to create conditions in which I can do my best work. In educational institutions with five hundred pupils or high schools with three thousand, it is true that someone must strategize about the movement of pupils through the building, about adequate numbers of teachers to cover classes, know about how to turn on the heat in the absence of the custodian and indeed be conversant with computers, police stations, and nutritionists. Excellent principals create comfortable, safe environments where experienced teachers can work their magic. At their most perceptive, principals should be able to lure talent (identify it through resumes, interviews, and then conduct discreet raids on other schools) to get topflight staff. The best principals understand that outstanding teachers are touchy, often slightly nutty people who are obsessed with the teaching role and frequently with the subject that they teach. As such, they can be highly dramatic and demanding but they also have the ability to blow smoldering embers in maturing brains into incandescence by making teaching skill a form of artistry in which imagining and (attempting, while dreaming) helping to create journeys through time and space. Great teachers are shamans. As much as I support the teacher's union, they forget that great teachers are not bound by contracts or machines that clock their goings and comings. Great principals understand that they need a wide latitude in which to operate and these principals aid and abet them because they trust them.

Perhaps Mr. Sklar saw something special in me as I told my stories in his assembly. He did not know whether I could teach, maintain discipline, or write coherent lesson plans, but he gambled, feeling "sure." And I did not disappoint.

My favorite story about him relates to a gloomy Monday morning when the class entered the room and I discovered that our class pet, a guinea pig, was dead. I am ashamed about my reaction because I acted like a pet-owner, not an educational leader. After all, I had provided the big, roomy cage that I had found in a poultry market, made frequent trips to the pet store for those pellets he ate, and cleaned his cage more than the kids did.

I screamed, dropped my books and handbag, and dashed across the hall to Mr. Sklar's office. I burst in yelling, "Our guinea pig is dead!" By this time, I had frightened the children, and they had begun to wail. Mr. Sklar was wonderful. He rushed into my classroom, and amid the general uproar, he picked up the dead pet and carried it out. I collapsed in my chair and tried to compose myself. Finally, we put our coats away and began the morning's activities. Things were returning to normal when Mr. Sklar reappeared.

He gathered the children around him and began to talk about death. He related the guinea pig's death to the cycle of life and talked about how pets were first young and cuddly, then mature and strong, but like all the things in the world, they got older and eventually died. He said that it was good to remember playing with our furry animal and talking to him and enjoying him. As a young teacher, I listened and learned something about comforting and calming children who had been frightened. During that visit, he was modeling a gentle concern and a sense of responsibility for their well-being that taught me a lesson. I know that he comforted us all, and when he left I was grateful that he was my principal. Not long after, he left the school. It is significant that he left our disadvantaged community to become principal of the school ranked number one in reading and math achievement in New York. This was P.S. 40 at Stuyvesant Town, a middle-class enclave on the east side of Manhattan. Although several of our best teachers elected to go with him (and yes, he did ask me), I chose to remain in Harlem.

The years that followed were the years of decentralization, Oceanville-Brownsville, and educational militancy. My school was part of the I.S. 201 complex so we were on the front lines of the struggle. Most of the African American and the white teachers in my school supported community control of the schools. In fact, at one point, P.S. 68 teachers defied the union and kept the school open during a strike by the New York teachers. Our principal at that time was an efficient, Caucasian woman named Jeanette Hunneau, who lived in Queens. She became a hero because during the period of the strike, she chose to stay in the Hotel Theresa to be near the school. Now the Theresa, a grand old lady of the Harlem Renaissance, had fallen on hard times during the 1960s.

Those were the years when crowds of men lined the sidewalks on Lenox Avenue with no jobs to go to and the population of white students at Rice High School, a Catholic boys' school on 124th Street, had begun to dwindle. Harlem was in the grip of a plague fueled by illegal drugs and high rates of crime. The Harlem of jazz clubs and café society was shutting down as the streets became unsafe. We watched Miss Hunneau striding down the street, our fingers crossed behind our backs, and sighed with relief when she turned up each morning, unharmed. She was stern, demanding, no-nonsense, but essentially kind. She didn't know the first thing about black culture, rock and roll, or social activism but she was respectful of parents, knew plenty about the teaching of reading, and came into classrooms to observe teachers and gave them carefully written evaluations of what she saw. She belonged to that class of elderly maiden ladies who seldom smiled, never showed favoritism, whose tread on the staircase frightened both teachers and students. I liked her a lot. Her generation was similar to those Irish ladies that I had encountered when I went to school in Brooklyn. They were lifelong educators. They understood the craft of teaching, maintained tight control of their classes, terrified parents with their formality and some of them infuriated parents with their condescension. Their pupils showed various levels of skill, but I never saw students who could not read and when the teacher rapped on the desk, the class became quiet. My school years under the tutelage of such women were uneventful and unremarkable. I learned everything that I was supposed to learn. I didn't know until I became part of the system that there was an "underside" to the school system that I could not see.

Principals were complicit in this system. Even though the system had competent teachers, and even though there were many bright students, Harlem junior high schools, like most minority schools, emptied into second-rate high schools. I have talked to many, many black professionals who had single-minded parents who had to fight long and hard to get them into college-bound programs. I remember that the junior high where I taught emptied into Central Commercial High School (practically everyone who graduated went there). They would be trained for clerical and commercial jobs. Boys were encouraged to go to Automotives High School or Westinghouse High in Brooklyn to learn a trade. I cannot forget my brother Jimmy, who was told at the end of his senior year that he could not graduate because he had not taken a foreign language. Please understand that at that time guidance counselors were not "guiding" and the required curriculum was a mystery. I remembered sitting down with a counselor at Eastern District High School (in Brooklyn) in my senior year as she totaled up my credits and I learned that I would graduate. In three years at Eastern I had never talked to a counselor.

The relentless testing and other missteps of the current Department of Education are recent attempts to correct a failed system. Major educational reform harks back to *Brown v. Board of Education* in 1954. This landmark decision made integrated schools a condition of equality in America but the major battles were fought in the South. Where integration occurred in the North, social class still kept the poor separated from the middle class. Communities like Harlem did not get integrated. At the same time, a recognition that minority students deserved worthy role models to emulate, was seen as a motivating factor in encouraging achievement. In African American communities like my school there developed a growing demand for principals who were members of minority groups. As a child growing up in Brooklyn, I had had teachers who were almost exclusively Irish. In the nineteen forties, when we moved to Fort Greene we qualified for public housing because my father worked in the Brooklyn Navy Yard. In my new school, P.S. 67, I encountered my first Jewish teacher. She wore a fur coat to school, wore perfume, and gold jewelry. By the time I began teaching in 1961, Jewish teachers were in the majority, both as teachers and administrators.

In 1960s Harlem, at P.S. 68, we got out first black principal, Mr. John Nailor, a golfer and a gentleman. Fortunately, ours was a well-run school and he did not have to patrol the hallways with a baseball bat like his famous counterpart in New Jersey. P.S. 68 was a stable school with a large number of effective senior teachers, many of them black males. We also had a large number of really superior female teachers. I remember Sarah Barber, the daughter of the famous sports columnist Red Barber, who was a gifted early childhood specialist, and Eloise Anderson, an alumnus of the legendary Katherine Dunham Dance Company, who excelled in teaching language arts. Later on, talented young women would have a chance to go to law school or medical school so they could look beyond teaching as they contemplated career paths. Mr. Nailor was the kind of principal who encouraged you to drop in to discuss problems. He was soft-spoken and dignified, a kindly "grandfather" figure that many of the children did not have in their lives, so he was universally loved. I could see the boys watching him and, I think, measuring themselves against him. I never saw him lose his temper and his rational approach to solutions showed a way of handling problems that was worth emulating. There was an unspoken bond of trust between Mr. Nailor and me. I liked his "style" and he liked mine. That we were both African Americans was a part of it. But more than that, he let me know that he approved of my classroom and my teaching. I believe that all good principals let you know that you are meeting their standards as a professional. There are job evaluations at the end of the year and an occasional note after a well-received assembly program, but there is a cordiality, a friendliness that a principal should exhibit, so that staff members know that he or she knows what an asset you are. I can remember the principal of a junior high school where I taught for a year. He had three or four assistant principals so he was never seen in the building. In fact he would make a "progress" around the school once a year. We were all warned that he was coming. Like a king, he would enter the classroom, survey the students (many of them had never seen him before) and then solemnly he would shake the teacher's hand and disappear. I don't think that he spoke. I remember how awed we all were. In a while I shall compare him with my all-time favorite principal. What a difference! Unfortunately, I did not get to know Mr. Nailor better because I soon left to teach at Rutgers University.

Since this chapter is about principals, we must fast-forward fourteen years to the time that I returned to the New York public school system. The first school to which I was assigned was nightmarish. It was in Harlem, and I was told that I was the third teacher to approach this class because the others had quit. I hated that school. It was a new building but cold, dark, with hallways where there seemed to be many corners or blind alleys. You were always turning corners not sure of what lay beyond. Since I always worked late in my classroom, the place was spooky. For the first time I met a custodian who leered at me, so I felt unsafe. And the principal was an African American female, very cold, very correct, and very difficult. I had to buy my roll book in order to keep attendance records. There were no supplies or money available for supplies. I was scandalized and was reduced to borrowing paper and pencils from other teachers. Believe it or not I only lasted one week in that horrible place. The children were outrageous and out of control, however, I realized that in time order could be restored. It was a first-grade class, but they had few skills. When I examined the permanent records (that followed the students from class to class), I found that this was what teachers call "a monster class." All the problems had been put in one room. A significant number of them were repeating first grade and one young man was in first grade for the third time. At that time, this was illegal. If a student was "left back" one time, the current teacher had to promote the student the next year, whether learning had taken place or not. I was very troubled because the student in question was well behaved but seemed unable to understand what was going on. Obviously, he should be tested. I went to the principal immediately and asked how a child could be repeating first grade twice. All I can say is that the principal looked at me, her eyes narrowing and she said that she would have more information the next day. Well guess what! When she entered my class, she took me aside and told me that I had been excessed. This meant I no longer had a job in that school. I didn't know exactly what she was up to, but it was clear that I was "trouble." Let me tell you something! My negative feelings about this woman had nothing to do with the fact that she was a black female like me. I have known and served with some outstanding black female principals in Harlem, among them Dellora Hercules, Jewel Welsh, and Ella Jackson. These were gifted educators who created schools where standards were high and performance met expectations.

Indeed, Ella Jackson had been pursuing a law degree at a time when there were few financial supports for gifted minority students. She began teaching in the school system when all hope of financial support disappeared. (I understood the bruising costs of law school because in graduate school, when I had to pay tuition, it was a choice between paying fees or going without light and gas for a while. We all have stories like this to tell.) After retirement, Jewel Welsh and Dellora Hercules both taught in local colleges, delighted to prepare a new generation of young professionals.

Since I had been excessed, I used my lunch period to throw my belongings into my car. I thought about the fact that here was a school, in the 1980s, with no books or paper or teaching aides (i.e., chalk). Something was wrong and I just wanted to get out. Saying good-bye to the class was painful. I was failing them. But it was clear that I couldn't help them either. So I escaped.

My experience with principals improved greatly when I was assigned to a middle- class school in the Bronx. The personnel officer at the Board had asked if I was willing to take an assignment in a school where there were few African American teachers. This largely Italian school had begun busing black and Hispanic children, and the district office was attempting to diversify the faculty. Near Pelham Parkway, this was a neighborhood of compact brick homes, tiny front gardens bursting with flowers and generally well-behaved children. Substitute teachers were not afraid to come to this school. Indeed, if a student was giving me problems, I could go into the office, call the child's mother and in a short time, she would be in my classroom. The teacher was respected and the kid was in trouble. An interesting aspect of this new situation was that this school was at the edge of the Albert Einstein Medical School complex. Most of the foreign doctors who were on fellowships sent their children to our school so we had bright local kids and super bright foreign kids from France, Japan, China, India, and Israel. This school was so delightful to work in it was known as "The Country Club" at the district office. When I began working there the school had no principal. However, the Head Teacher, Marilyn Maloff was top-notch. I had an unforgettable moment on my first day. There had been an overabundance of kindergarteners that year and it was necessary to open a new class. So I was given the day to fix up my classroom. I arranged the tables and chairs. Then I began to decorate my bulletin board (inside the classroom), because I knew that it was the first thing that my children would see. I created an autumn scene from poster paper with a big greeting of welcome. There was an apple tree, squirrels, and a school building. The head teacher slipped into the room as I worked and watched me for a while. When she came over to greet me she said, "You don't know what a pleasure it is to watch a professional working. Welcome!" Tears rolled down my cheeks. We both knew that it would go well.

Getting to P.S. 108 was killing, but once there, it was heaven. I had to drive on three highways in order to reach the Bronx and the Bruckner Expressway was under construction so there were times when I arrived late. But my wonderful head teacher/acting principal had the children waiting, soothed my anxiety, and eased me into the day's work. She commented that her husband was having the same difficulty getting to work in Manhattan. She could have yelled about keeping the poor children sitting idly or the usual comment that administrators make, "You just have to get up earlier." She didn't. So I blossomed as a teacher. Soon I was putting on elaborate assembly programs. My favorite was an adaptation called "Our Multicultural Kindergarten." A little research revealed that there were nine different ethnic groups represented in my kindergarten (including Albanian and African). The school had exciting festivals in which we all took part. Imagine! In the largest school yard I had ever seen, our annual Sports Day began with a fifth grader circling the yard carrying a lighted torch as the music from the movie *Chariots of Fire* played and everybody cheered. There was a district storytelling contest, a Halloween parade through all the classrooms, and parties galore. One the last day of school, the custodian, who drove a jeep and had just gotten his law degree, served the faculty tasty mimosas made of champagne and orange juice. This same daredevil went from classroom to classroom carrying tumblers of Irish coffee (whiskey) on the last day before Christmas vacation. (The head teacher was none the wiser.)

The school finally got an assistant principal who speedily became a principal. His name was Victor Crecco. He was Italian, like the District Superintendent Frank Arricale and the Deputy Superintendent Bob Constanza. I adored them all. Arricale endeared himself to me by coming to my classroom and actually reading a story to the children, then having a discussion with them. Master politician that he was, he further endeared himself to me when he told the assembled parents at a PTA meeting that they were lucky to have the best kindergarten teacher in the city of New York, Dr. Jean Lloyd. He then got s standing ovation. His deputy, Bob Constanza became my friend because we both adored opera and his buddy was Franco Corelli of Metropolitan Opera fame. Corelli was as handsome as a movie star, six feet tall and looked sublime in tights. Bob would come to my classroom during my lunch period and bring tapes of Corelli singing arias from *Tosca*. Need I say that these were among my happiest years as a teacher. On parents' conference night, if I had twenty-seven children, twenty-seven mothers and twenty-seven fathers appeared, delighted that their kids were in my class (the mothers were happy, but some of the fathers wouldn't look me in the eye). I was aware of a historical strain of racism in some Italians that went back to an earlier time when Italians and blacks competed for the same low-skilled jobs. When my family moved to Queens, we bought our house from an Italian family who was fleeing the influx of black families. Of course it is clear now that this was orchestrated by the real estate companies who then sold our house for top dollar. Nevertheless, African Americans have a sometimes-tense relationship with Italian Americans. The Italians either embrace you or dislike you. I am reminded of my favorite Bronx family, the Salvatores and the wonderful eggplant Parmesan that Angela makes for me. I have had several of her six children in my class and they were invariably brilliant and lovable. As for those Italian fathers who don't look me in the eye during parent conferences . . . didn't matter! (Those Italian mothers fought to get their kids in my class knowing that their kids would get a solid education.)

Mr. Crecco, my principal, had spent his early career as a fifth grade teacher in Harlem. He was funny and wise and kind. He enjoyed telling me that one of the reasons that his black students felt comfortable with him was because his hair was kinky like theirs. I always remarked that as an Italian from southern Italy, his ancestors lived close to Africa. There was obviously a story there!

My favorite story about Mr. Crecco centered on a bulletin board that I did. The bulletin board inside my classroom was spectacular, covering the wall from the floor to a space above my head. The bulletin board in the hallway was about four feet by seven. As I developed my reading program using the model of the current favorites, the "infant schools" of New Zealand (the genesis of the "whole Language programs" at Bank Street College and Columbia University), I wanted to show off my children's skills. We had begun to teach reading in a way that allowed the child to puzzle out words based on what they already knew and what they inferred, logically and from pictures. They were allowed to write using what we called "invented spelling." Because of their continuing reading activities, they would learn appropriate spelling in first grade. Actually, because they were in a "print-rich" environment we felt they would soon correct themselves. But the crucial thing was to prevent them from becoming self-conscious about writing by correcting them and pointing out mistakes. This would inhibit their flow of expression.

When I finished my monthly bulletin board, I asked the principal to have a look because the children were expressing their own thoughts in a way that was generally intelligible. "Jean" he said, "The words are misspelled. Some parents have seen the board and they are upset." What was immediately clear to me was an age-old problem with principals. They rarely understood anything about kindergarten. (Remember, Mr. C had been a fifth grade teacher). He didn't understand the triumph of getting five-year-olds to express their thoughts in writing. I explained the damage I could do if I made them afraid to write because the words might be misspelled. Mr. Crecco thought about it and figured out a solution. I was to write a "blurb" or statement explaining what I was doing and place it next to the bulletin board. In a few lines I explained the idea of "invented spelling" and that was the end of that. The parents were delighted that their children were writing in kindergarten.

Mr. Crecco continued to be my favorite principal even though he would sometimes appear at my door, when a teacher was absent, with a student, and tell me that he was allowing the young man to be my "helper" for the day. What he really meant was that some kid was torturing the substitute teacher and had to be removed. During lunch Crecco's admirers would sit around and complain (while laughing). When a teacher sent a kid to the office for an infraction, the kid returned to the class to tell how the principal had pulled a quarter out of his ear or how the principal had taught him/her a magic trick. The kids liked him as much as we did. A much-loved principal creates such goodwill that he/she can impose on teachers to do things that they really don't want to be bothered with. Mr. Crecco might ask you to serve on a committee to choose a new textbook or evaluate the new math program that we had begun using. We never refused these tasks. He made school fun.

More importantly our principal was wise enough to respect the skills of his staff and sought to share their strengths with their peers. During one of our staff development days, when the children went home after a half-day in school, I was delighted to give a presentation explaining how I carried out my reading and writing program. Copies of the children's work were passed around, and I was able to explain some of my strategies. For example, as I called out each child's name during attendance, the child was required to answer, "I am here." From the first day I encouraged them to speak in sentences. The payoff in June was that they also wrote in sentences. A small activity like this might be a revelation to a new teacher, so I was happy to share many pedagogical ideas.

I have so many wonderful memories of "The Crecco Years." Imagine the situation of leaving the building at three o'clock. The children would be sitting in the lunchroom at the tables, waiting for the buses. They would be talking, but not too loudly. Mr. Crecco would be patrolling the area but talking to students, doing the quarter trick, just socializing with his charges. He had the kind of personality that calms children so there was no disorder. There was that "you know what I expect" look that stopped boys who tumbled off the benches, ready to wrestle. It was like a "cool down" time. I never rushed out of the building. I left slowly.

Another proud memory is that one of my kindergarteners was a winner in the Women's History Month contest sponsored by the New York Borough President's office. My kid had made an enchanting picture of a female astronaut floating in space, and she appeared in the local paper with Mayor Ed Koch. Mr. Crecco let our winner go around to all the classrooms and show her painting and the Olympic-style medal that she won. Her mother was thrilled.

When I began my teaching career, outstanding teachers often became principals. Indeed, principals were able to go into classrooms and teach lessons, cover for absent teachers, and conduct staff development seminars. At the time I left the system, staff development was being conducted by literacy coaches, math coaches, and others. Principals seemed to be building managers and coordinators of programs. My old elementary school now has two assistant principals and the grades are no longer prekindergarten to fifth grade but have become pre-K to eighth grade. Considering the chaos and the low achievement levels of the middle schools this is probably a good thing. Students are carefully trained from preschool now in acceptable behavior. The internalization of the norms and values of the school is taking place with the help of supervisory staff, building security guards, and police personnel so that sixth, seventh, and eighth graders have a better chance at rewarding school experiences. Whatever works!

When I returned to Harlem after my Bronx experience I was at the top of my game. I was ready to teach reading to my kindergarteners and to share my skills with my peers. Getting into a school was hard because as a tenured professional, after my district superintendent released me, I could "bump" another teacher from any school where I applied. This did not endear me to principals. My doctorate did not endear me to the other teachers. Remember that when I entered my new school, only fourteen percent of students were reading on grade level in my school.

Rather than critically evaluating the three building principals that I worked with in Harlem, a cheerless exercise at best, I feel more comfortable in discussing the characteristics that I think top-notch principals must have in order to have schools that perform at a high level and children who thrive. Here we go!

CHARACTERISTICS AND PERFORMANCE OF OUTSTANDING PRINCIPALS

1. *Providing safety*—The most important job that a principal has is to develop a safe environment, whatever it takes: security guards, locks on classroom doors, police sweeps of the building, the block, the neighborhood, local parents working in the school in professional and paraprofessional roles.

2. *Having a level of competency*—Principals are responsible for the quality of school curriculum, and they must organize activities within the school. However, the day of the teaching principal is probably over. Expertise in teaching reading and math skills is creating a new kind of professional (math and literacy coaches). Ties with Columbia University and

Bank Street College and Hunter College have led to teams of professionals on site, training teachers, and staff. The principal must be involved in planning, implementing, and evaluating curricula but is rarely in the classroom teaching. However, principals must still oversee, stay late, and take work home. Records, reports, evaluations must be addressed in a timely way. Principals must meet with teaching staff regularly to be aware of student academic progress throughout the grades. The principal has final responsibility for the improvement of pupil attendance, punctuality, and their physical and mental health. Principals are now like sports coaches and corporation CEOs. If school performance does not improve, they lose their jobs.

3. *Not hiding in the office*—Principals should be in the hallways, in the school yard, in the lunchroom. Sure, there are assistant principals but the person who is ultimately responsible should be "out there," on the case.

4. *Creating the best staff of professionals possible*—This will sound harsh but incompetent teachers must go. Initially, they should be given assistance and more training. But at a certain point, they should be asked to move on. I believe that it takes five years to develop a competent professional. One improves year after year. But if a teacher after ten or fifteen years still has no control, still cannot produce a quiet classroom, still cannot walk the class down the hallway without major disruptions, still cannot document improvements in student performance, still cannot teach a class before other pedagogues, it's time to go. One of the saddest things I have seen is teachers who get moved from grade to grade, from failure to failure, and eventually wind up teaching kindergarten or pre-K (where frankly the most proficient teachers are needed). My heart goes out to the children who must sit in chaotic classrooms day after day, in anguish because of the noise, lack of stability, and feel unable to concentrate. Five years is a generous amount of time in which to strategize for

success. We must always remember the children and our job
to educate them.

5. *Recognizing that the best teachers are "stars"*—They should
be given merit pay because they provide a unique service.
While holding them to high professional standards (i.e., they
cannot drift in late), the principal should let them know that
they are cherished. Formal letters should go into personal
files, praise should be meted out at faculty meetings, and top
teachers in the school should be selected by their faculties
for financial rewards based on mastery of skills in teaching,
high levels of student achievement and/or improvement of
pupil performance. However, where master teachers become
disruptive, and abuse their charismatic power, like unprin-
cipled principals, they should be removed (transferred) with
proper documentation and union collaboration. This reminds
me of the medieval kings in England, when the most powerful dukes had the clout to challenge and revolt against them.
I accept the principal as a legitimate chief executive who
collaborates with faculty but he/she should be free to direct
and lead.

6. *Maintaining high moral standards*—Having sexual relations
with staff is nuts. Relationships within the school that even the
students know about (and students know quite a lot) sets the
wrong tone, compromises ethical standards, and frequently
leads to embarrassment and trouble. Avoid, avoid, avoid!

7. *Celebrating ethnicity within the community*—The principal
must help to celebrate the ethnic backgrounds of the students
and teachers. With so many legal (and illegal) immigrants
coming into our nation, the schools have an important role
to play in teaching newcomers about their roles as future citizens. America is a country where festivals and holidays are
important civic events. Thanksgiving Day parades around
the nation show us at our most hospitable and welcoming.
At the same time we have an opportunity to reveal our history and traditions to newcomers. The Saint Patrick's Day

Parade, an Irish celebration, is made of many non-Irish groups who take part and enjoy the day. My favorite is the African American members of the armed forces who march yearly. These veterans fought in World War II (i.e., the 369th Regiment). I always scream and yell to let them know they are not forgotten and how much I value their contribution, their heroism, and valor in protecting all Americans. Knowledge of student body ethnicities will guide in choosing assembly guests and graduation speakers. Let the principal invite worthy role models for the students to meet. Because many of our newest immigrants are Muslims, holidays offer opportunities to celebrate their traditions as well as those of Jews and Christians, encouraging interfaith tolerance. One year a Jewish teacher in our school made "latkes," a holiday treat for her class. It is not necessary to discuss religious doctrine to enjoy delicious food. Sharing fosters respect and goodwill. And finally, I strongly suggest that the principal have links with community organizations. The local political clubs are happy to donate computers and software to the school. Banks are generous with graduation prizes and will come to talk about preparation for careers. I am sorry to say that it was only after I had left my school that I learned that the famous African American poet, Langston Hughes, lived down the block. No one else seemed to know this either. Imagine the poetry readings, the ceremonies to honor him, the curriculum that we could have built around his literary contributions. The children could have met him, interviewed him, and asked him questions. Later, when I left P.S. 68 to go to Rutgers to teach sociology, a student told me that he knew Claude Brown, the author of the seminal, *Manchild in the Promised Land.* (1965) He came to our classroom and gave the students an exciting experience. Every community offers such riches. The principal can help expose students to them. They have a unique opportunity to enrich the lives of students.

Nuts and Bolts—The Principal as Manager or CEO

We have said that safety and security of children and staff are the most important concerns of the principal. But there are many areas where skillful management is necessary. The principal must strive for improvements in the physical and mental health of students. The wholesome social interaction of students, must be encouraged (i.e., gang activity, drug use must be prevented from developing.) Where they exist they must be discouraged and eliminated as rapidly and as forcefully as possible. A strong sports program should be developed for all classes and all ages. Music programs and art activities with the guidance of professionals are mandatory curriculum assets. However the bottom line is improvement in pupil achievement. The successful tenure of any principal is judged by the improvement shown in pupil achievement.

In a course on "School Management" Andrew G. Donaldson (1985), who became the first black district superintendent, discussed the diverse relationships a principal must have within the school. To improve staff effectiveness, the school manager must interact with:

1. Supervisory Staff
2. Maintenance Staff
3. Custodial Staff
4. Pedagogical Staff
5. Guidance Staff
6. Pupil Personnel Services Staff
7. Paraprofessional Staff
8. Auxiliary Staff (Aides)
9. Transportation Staff
10. Food Services Staff
11. Clerical Staff
12. Professional Resource People
13. Service Personnel (i.e., Security Personnel)
14. Volunteer Personnel

The Principal's Sense of Mission

Any principal in any school anywhere in the United States can give you a mission statement (i.e., goals). They begin each term with a reference to the mission of their school. It is referred to constantly in faculty meetings. It dances trippingly off the tongue of principals. However in June the mission of the school is seldom accomplished. It is rarely mentioned. The mission statement is made up of platitudes, stock phrases, and empty words. Rarely do principals assess the degree to which the school's mission has been accomplished. Would assessing the success of the school's mission monthly make a difference? What about daily?

11

An Unavoidable Ritual—
Kindergarten Graduation

WHY ARE THEY GRADUATING? I don't know. They are not even leaving the school. In earlier years when we accepted an overflow of Hispanic children from Washington Heights (some schools had as many as eleven kindergartens) our June graduations signaled a return to their neighborhood schools. Even before that, kindergarten graduation had been institutionalized as a "cute" ceremony although only a handful of children would be going off to Catholic school or private school to begin first grade. This annual event made the principal look good, was enormously festive and gave the children a chance to show some of the things they had learned. The positives have always outweighed the negatives. Let's face it, kindergarten graduation has always been a ritual primarily of importance to parents. In my Harlem school, it has gotten so ostentatious that parents have been known to hire stretch limos for the occasion. Little children wear corsages, are given bouquets of flowers, and the parents association sold school rings (with stones in them). Please remember that my school services a disadvantaged population. Every child in the school gets free lunch. While some of them live in chaotic households and some come to school wearing summer clothes in wintertime, on the day of kindergarten graduation, excess reigns. Parents want a chance to feel proud and see their children as successful. Mothers get their hair done in fanciful braids and curls and even fathers who are generally absent, turn up with gifts and plans for trips to Chuck E. Cheese or local restaurants.

The annual ceremony begins at about 9:00 a.m. with the children marching into the auditorium to the strains of Elgar's "Pomp and Circumstance." Because parents vote for it each year, the children wear academic gear, girls in white robes and mortarboards, and the boys in blue. These must be purchased, not rented. Under the robes I could see white socks with frilly lace cuffs and new patent leather shoes. Many of the girls were also wearing beautiful new dresses, with tulle and satin bows. Most of the boys were wearing suits with long pants and expensive-looking ties.

In past years, clearing the aisles of parents with camcorders had been a problem, but this year they were filming from the two sections at the sides of the auditorium. The overflow was so great that the sliding back wall was open and the parent's section extended into the gym next door. My class led the procession this year, and they were properly solemn as they walked to the end of each row and spaced themselves so that three children did not end up in the same seat. We were not so lucky with the Pledge of Allegiance. Because there have been recent graduations without the Pledge, the music teacher laid down the law. There would be a Pledge or he would know why. The assemblage mumbled their way through it. But "The Star-Spangled Banner" was depressing. It reminded me of baseball games where the loudspeaker blares out the music, and the people are just standing, impatient to begin. In truth, the national anthem is impossible to sing. The melody goes up too high so, at a certain point, those that were singing begin to drop out. Every year I promise myself that I will lobby for "My Country, 'Tis of Thee," but in the press of activities, I forget. This year, the kids struggled through it. The parents gave up. "My Country, 'Tis of Thee" is lovely, lively, and learnable.

The next song was what is called "The Negro National Anthem," "Lift Ev'ry Voice and Sing." It is sung in churches and inner-city schools all over the United States. The lyricist is James Weldon Johnson, a prolific poet, writer, and educator of the early twentieth century (1900). His brother, J. Rosamond Johnson, composed the music. This anthem is not easy to sing either, but it has a terrific rhythmic beat so even if the words are difficult, the children are carried along by the pulses and the consonants:

Sing a song full of the faith that our dark past has taught us,
Sing a song full of the hope that the present has brought us . . .

It's also long, but the kids have sung it so often they can do a creditable job with it. My class, especially the Hispanic children, loved it.

At this point the classes began individual presentations. My class was up first. Happy to get it over with, I led the children up on the stage. They stood on a line taped across the stage. I knew that it was going to be "a piece of cake." Why? Because I stress choral speaking and oral presentations. My kids, at the drop of a hat, recite poems for holidays like Halloween, Mother's Day, Valentine's Day, and Groundhog's Day. Sometimes I take them to the office and they recite for the secretaries or school visitors. Like all four- and five-year-olds, they never make mistakes, recite exactly as they have been taught, and they have an advantage that older children do not have. They are never nervous. With the teacher standing there, they are little "show-offs" delighted to have the stage. I usually say, "One, Two, Three, Go!" and they are off. Standing proudly on the stage, three children did a welcome to parents, teachers, and students. Then they all presented a charming little poem, "When I Was One":

When I was One,
I had just begun.
When I was Two,

I was nearly new.

When I was Three,

I was hardly Me.

When I was Four,

I was not much more.

When I was Five,

I was hardly alive.

But now I am Six, I'm as clever as clever.

So I think I'll be six now for ever and ever.

　　　　—A. A. Milne, 1927

We always add:

After all . . . I'm going to first grade. I will succeed!

(Much applause)

This poem was created by the author of the Winnie-the-Pooh stories. We get "cutesy pooh" with this one. The children hold up the correct number of fingers with each numeral and when we get to "I'm as clever as clever," we hold up our chins and shake our fingers at the audience and finally we tap our temples, "So I think I'll be six . . ." Girls curtsey. Boys bow.

The other three classes contributed recitations and songs. They were most effective if the teachers had rehearsed them thoroughly. After the ceremonies were over the teachers marched the children back to their classrooms where commendations were to be given out and cake and juice were to be enjoyed. If we assume that each child had one or more parents and aunts, grandparents, and other siblings present, the noise and general confusion were predictable. Also, after the ceremonies, the children were wild. Maybe they had behaved long enough. So the teacher had to assume control and restore order. Once the children returned to the classroom, the teachers were instructed to give awards to high achievers. These were in addition to diplomas that were provided and signed by the principal. The problem is that unruly children frequently have unruly parents. As I stood at the front of the room, I would stop and wait for quiet but found it difficult to speak above the noise.

The school gave awards to children with the highest reading scores on the state mandated tests. Their test, Early Childhood Literary Assessment System (ECLAS), categorizes children from level 1 to level 6. Level 1 and 2 means that the child is at a "readiness" or kindergarten level. Level 5 and 6 means that the child reads on a second grade level. (Level 6 is the end of second grade.) I had three children reading at level 6, three children reading on level 5 and six children reading on level 4.

It seemed extremely important to recognize those little kindergarten children who could show such progress in one year. It would be significant to acknowledge that, in addition to my help, these children had the support of parents who worked with us and were deeply involved in their children's progress. I can remember other years where I was careful to give every child some kind of recognition (i.e., for learning to tie one's shoelaces). But I have changed my mind. It is simply not helpful to equate an award for best table cleanups with an award to a child who can read a story in the newspaper at five or six years old. Without lecturing them, I wanted parents to see that there were things that they needed to be doing. And sure enough, the parents who did not help with homework (they do the assignment for the child . . . you can tell), who never come to parent conferences, these parents became angry. An undercurrent of hostility grew and the noise level began to grow. I was not surprised. At one point, I crossed my arms and said, "Parents, I have an orderly classroom. My children do not talk when I am talking. I'll wait for quiet." A very aggressive grandmother appeared at my side and asked, "Is Perry getting an award?" "No, but I want to give him a storybook as a present, for summer reading." "Well, we're leaving," she said, "I have to go to work." And she walked out. As Ms. Acevedo, my educational assistant and I began dismissing the children and their parents, in my head I was mumbling, "Sure, Calvin should have gotten an award for getting into the most fights and if Keyana was going to get an award it would be for never doing her homework." The parents were angry with me for failing to make their children look good on this special day but I decided that, since I was moving into my last year before retirement, pretending that all was well, was counterproductive. The game had changed. Our children are expected to learn to read in kindergarten now. Yet not all parents are "getting with the program." We are a school of about four hundred pupils yet when we have a parents association meeting, we feel successful if twenty-five parents show up. We have family Thanksgiving dinners in school and the turnout is not large. As educators we know that the relationship between children's success in school and the degree of parent involvement is high so that giving rewards to the friendliest children, even the most cooperative, is beside the point. In my class, the friendliest and the most cooperative are also the best readers. On the June report cards, the stark truth is there. If a child has not learned his/her phonic sounds (the sound that each letter has), if the child cannot sound out a word that is unfamiliar, if a child rarely turns in homework, if a child is a bully and frightens other children . . . and if parents or caregivers never respond to letters from the school . . . now is the time to grasp the fact that something is wrong. Perhaps summer school will help. For some therapy is another option.

Dear Parents: If your child does not have a successful first year, I can only share the blame. You are at fault too. I feel terrible when a child is struggling and not succeeding but this is not the result of an inexperienced teacher or an uncaring educator. I have forty years of teaching experience. That counts for something. So I wanted to say to those angry parents, "You need to be angry with yourselves!

"Why don't you check your child's book bag daily for communications from the school? Why are notes never signed or returned? Why don't you come to parent-teacher conferences? When the class is going on a trip why do I have to call you at 9:30 a.m. to get a verbal OK so that Sally can go when I have sent you three notices? You may not be able to check subtraction homework, but you can ask to see the completed assignment so that you know that the work has been done and later ask for a workshop on subtraction so that you can learn to help."

I know parents are harassed and frustrated by work, by lack of work, by damaged relationships, but if your kindergartener's report card has "Needs Improvement" next to reading readiness and mathematics, there is work to be done. I understand that at kindergarten graduation, parents do not want their relatives to know that something is amiss at school. However, I think of the deeply troubled young man in my class who, at six years, cries three or four times daily (and believe me, kindergarten boys do not like to be seen crying), who fights constantly, who knows very few alphabet letters and who can read not at all. When I spoke to this child's mother about a free service whereby we could have a social worker counsel her child, the mother refused the service saying, "My child is a happy child." She does not suspect that I know that the happy child's brother, a third grader, was not promoted last year. This may well be a situation where there are family secrets which the mother is afraid we will discover. Meanwhile, her children seem to be suffering.

Oh well, even though our "moving up" ceremony is another festival to be lived through, I am sure that it will continue. As E. R. Shipp commented in her column, "Graduations Shouldn't Go Sour," (2003) "It's an 'attaboy' and 'you go, girl' communal salute." Her column is addressing fifth graders and she is aware that the celebratory mood will be very different when many city kids are of high school age. She notes that one in five will drop out before graduating. Fifty percent of those who remain will take longer than four years to graduate. Of those who do not graduate, some will be in jail. Some will be dead. Such baleful facts put a different spin on events like our kindergarten graduation. The chance to stand up and be proud is closely related to years of monitoring, checking up, to conferencing with teachers, making sure that children are well fed, adequately rested, and healthy. "Moving up" is a joyous end to much hard work. I just wish they would lose the caps and gowns and class rings in kindergarten. A kiss and a hug would be fine!

12

When Death Occurs—
Comforting Children

IT IS A SAD fact that young children are exposed to death more frequently than we like to admit. In the not too distant past, mothers often died giving birth to brothers and sisters. On farms and plantations, mothers (free or in bondage), died of overwork as they helped to plow, milk, harvest, cook, clean, and raise families. Fathers died in accidents, in wars, in social conflicts. Disease took a heavy toll on every group. Today we are aware of the loss facing young children as their parents perish due to drugs, AIDS, diabetes, cancer, crime, or the ravages of war. Small children sit through funerals, stand at the graveside looking bereft and confused, or stand by the coffin where they are told to say good-bye to a loved one. In my class we had the sad experience of taking a mother, who was dying, on a class trip so that she could enjoy her child in the time that she had left. Over the years, we have had a large number of children who were being raised by grandparents because their mothers were deceased, incarcerated, or hospitalized. As teachers, we must comfort and help children who have been traumatized by death and the loss of one or both parents. How do we deal with such sadness?

The first thing for a teacher to understand is the terror that the child feels on learning that a parent, family member, or beloved caregiver has died. Children are frequently told that the deceased is gone, will never return, is "in heaven." In addition to feeling frightened and shocked by the disappearance of someone that the child cares for, a young child has no real conception of what death means. If Daddy is gone, does that mean that Mommy will be gone next? The child's sense of security is damaged and fear displaces certainty as the predictable world is replaced by the unknown. One of the worst mistakes that families make is to tell the child that the dead person has gone to sleep and is not going to wake up. The error is clear when the young child is afraid to go to sleep, fearful that he/she will not wake up.

We must remember that in the movies, especially in cartoons, animals fall off buildings, get blown up, sink in rivers, yet they reappear, dust themselves off and continue on. The indestructibility of cartoon characters might cause a five-year-old to think that if that "nutty coyote" can get blown up, then still be walking and talking, then perhaps the dead parent or friend will reappear too. "Gone forever" has no meaning for the child.

Yet it is clear that when death occurs, most of us go through stages of grief as we try to cope with loss. Elizabeth Kübler-Ross, a psychiatrist and educator, has been influential in examining these stages as well as in changing contemporary attitudes about the experience of death and the treatment of those who are dying (1969, 1997) (Kübler-Ross and Kessler, 2007).

Having worked in hospitals, medical schools, colleges, and hospices, Kübler-Ross saw a patterned reaction both in the dying and the bereaved. Such individuals:

"Went through similar stages. They started off with shock and denial, rage and anger, and then grief and pain. Later, they bargained with God. They got depressed, asking, 'Why me?' And finally they withdrew into themselves for a bit, separating themselves from others while hopefully reaching a stage of peace and acceptance."

Young children who are frightened and confused about what has happened often feel intense anger. On some level the child is blaming and thinking, "If you loved me, then you wouldn't leave me." Jodi Freeman (1991) a teacher for seventeen years found that many of her students had known someone who had died recently through events like "drowning, automobile accidents, drug overdoses, cancer, suicide, and murder." She concluded that in order to deal with the pain, sadness, and anger they were feeling, her whole class "needed to grieve." She came to class with "an armload of pillows." She seated the class in a circle on the carpet. She then asked her students, "What kind of feelings did you have when someone you knew died?" One student expressed his anger at his grandfather, who had committed suicide. Ms. Freeman asked the student to pick a pillow. She then tried to help him channel his feelings. She said, "Pretend the pillow is your grandfather . . . What would you like to say to him?" The young man said, "I miss you. And I'm mad you for killing yourself. I wanted a grandpa. I wanted to get to know you, and now I never can." The chance to express his feelings had some effect. He said good-bye and "gently laid the pillow aside."

A girl in Ms. Freeman's class had not attended her grandmother's funeral. We know that funerals serve an important function in the lives of those who are grieving. They allow us to share our grief as the loved one is remembered and wept over. A sense of closure comes as the rituals and ceremonies are enacted (the prayers, music, eulogy, quiet moments of reflection, and if it occurs, the trip to the cemetery). Because she had missed the funeral, the young girl decided to have a funeral in her class. She used the pillow together with a box, and after pretending to dig a grave, she gave her own eulogy, remembering her grandmother's life. The teacher noted that several students pounded out their anger using the beanbag chairs. Where children needed help in expressing their grief (to the deceased), the teacher said, "What do you wish (he'd/she'd) say to you?" Soon the children were comforting each other, even putting their arms around their classmates and talking to them. The teacher tactfully withdrew and began doing a jigsaw puzzle. As the healing progressed, some children, apparently feeling some relief, moved from talking about death to more general conversations.

Jacqueline Morison, who was my staff developer for District Three in New York, conducted workshops on Death Education for teachers and was very helpful in giving them suggestions about how they could comfort grieving children. Because many of the children in our schools witnessed frequent acts of violence, she helped us understand the effects of such occurrences. She pointed us to a report in *The New York Times* (Shuchman, 1991), where several experts who were interviewed about the effects of trauma concluded that children exposed to continual violence (in the home, in the street, in school) developed psychological problems including "depression, anxiety, behavior problems, and low self-esteem." Children may actually develop a form of post-traumatic stress disorder where they "reenact a horrifying event in repetitive, joyless play." Dr. Calvin Michael of the New York State Psychiatric Institute in Manhattan remarked that the trauma resulted from being in an environment where people were being hurt, shot at, or dying in the street. Dr. Michael used weekly therapy sessions to treat such children. Another health professional, Dr. Neal Halfon, the Director of the Center for the Vulnerable Child at Oakland Children's Hospital in California, worked with children who had witnessed at least one violent death. He said that "by age five they know 'that person across the street got blown away. I could get blown away.' When you think about this kind of assault on a child's psyche, you realize that there will have to be some mental health problems in these kids."

John Richters, a researcher at the National Institute of Mental Health in Bethesda, Maryland, reported on exposure to violence in a neighborhood school of Washington, DC. Interviews with children and their mothers revealed that six percent of the fifth and sixth graders had been shot at, and eleven percent had seen someone shot. Using national norms, Mr. Richters compared them with his survey group and found that the children he had studied were "three times more likely to have 'clinically significant psychological and psychiatric problems' than an average child."

Because the unresolved grief resulting from devastating experiences can "color a [child's] whole life," counseling with a trained professional offers hope to those scarred by violence and death. Dr. Spencer Eth, a psychiatrist, who headed a counseling service in Los Angeles where gang activity is constant, compared teenagers exposed to urban violence to "battle-weary soldiers" traumatized by combat. In addition to counseling, Dr. Eth encouraged his patients to draw pictures and talk about the horrors they had seen as part of the healing process.

Because Dr. Michael (New York Psychiatric Institute) believed that many strategies were useful in helping grieving children, and where there were enough individuals to form a group, he encouraged them to write scripts and make movies. For children not ready to communicate traumatic events, Dr. Michael bought a Nintendo system for his office. Using the game, he was often able to establish contact with withdrawn children and build the trust needed to begin the therapeutic process.

Dr. Elizabeth Kübler-Ross (1926–2004) made an enormous contribution to science, the social sciences, and education when she offered a more nuanced and humane way of handling the end of life for those who were dying. She was particularly effective in her discussion of the "unthinkable," the death of children. In *The Wheel of Life: A Memoir of Living and Dying* (1997) she noted that terminally ill children handled their situation better than many adults.

"Unlike older patients, the children had not accumulated layers of 'unfinished business.' They did not have a lifetime of botched relationships or a resume of mistakes. Nor did they feel compelled to pretend that everything was okay. They knew instinctively how sick they were, or that they were dying, and they did not hide their feelings about it."

She tells us about Tom, a child that she worked with at La Rabida Children's Hospital. He had serious kidney problems but was enraged at all the time he had to be in the hospital. Dr. Kübler-Ross took him outside the hospital and allowed him to throw rocks into a nearby lake. "Pretty soon," she said, "He was ranting about his kidney and all the other problems that prevented him from having the life of a normal little boy." Yet after twenty minutes he was changed. The doctor understood that all that she had done was to give him the chance to express his "pent-up" feelings.

THE LITERATURE OF CONSOLATION

The death of a beloved pet is an all too common occurrence in the lives of very young children. The loss of a cat or dog or hamster, fish, or bird is terribly painful to the child who has enjoyed and cared for the pet. There are a number of picture books about the death of family pets that offer some comfort to children. Such books can be used metaphorically to help them understand about the event of death in the case of a family member. One that I used was called *A Funeral for Whiskers* by Dr. Lawrence Balter. (1991) In addition to being a story that a parent can read to a child, Dr. Balter includes some helpful insights on the back cover of the book specifically for parents. He is aware of the difficulty of helping a child understand the notion of death. He is very conscious of the sense of power-lessness and anger that the child feels due to the loss. Dr. Balter stresses the importance of helping children to talk about their feelings during grieving. In the picture book story, Sandy notices that her cat is not very playful before school. Whiskers doesn't eat anything either. When Sandy is leaving, Whiskers doesn't climb up to the window to see her off. Later on, Mom takes Whiskers to the vet to see if she is all right. She leaves the cat, because the vet, Dr. Perkins, wants to do some tests and see what is wrong. When Sandy comes home, Mom tells her that the vet has called. Whis-kers, who was very old, has died. Sandy and Mom hug each other and sit on the couch and talk about Whiskers. "I don't want Whis-kers to be dead," says Sandy. At bedtime Mom and Dad help Sandy to get ready for bed. Sandy is distressed that the cat is not there to cuddle up on her bed. So Mom observes that the cat can't do that anymore but she will sit with Sandy to help her fall asleep. The next day, when Dad has gone to get the cat's body, Mom and Sandy draw pictures and get ready for Whisker's funeral. Mom has time to explain that a funeral is "a time when we say good-bye to someone who has died . . . when we remember nice things about them." Sandy doesn't want to say good-bye; she wants to play with her cat. Very patiently Mom explains about death. She reminds Sandy about a dead bird that they had found in the back yard. The bird could no longer fly. Mom gently describes the difference between being alive and not being alive. Sandy continues to protest. Mom is careful to say that Dad is bringing Whisker's body home for the funeral but it's just her body because "she isn't alive anymore." This book is excellent in anticipating the things that a child would say in trying to understand. Sandy wants to know if the cat will be scared to be buried all alone. Then she wants to know why she can't keep the cat in her room. Mom patiently responds to all the child's questions, and when Dad returns, they go outside to find a nice place to bury her. The family goes through the rituals of a funeral, and Sandy puts ribbons around the box on which she has drawn a picture and attaches a rubber spider that Whiskers liked to play with. Soon enough, Sandy is then anxious about Mom dying and Dad and Grandmother. Her mother calms her fears by reassuring her that they are all healthy and plan to be around for a long time. But she wisely adds, "All living things die someday." She mentions leaves, flowers, the fish at school . . . even people. There is much conversation between mother and daughter as the child copes with her cat's death. Her parents are ready to comfort and show that they care. Dad even brings home some pussy willows to plant at the grave. And mother finds some pictures of Whiskers to tack up in Sandy's room. She is encouraged to remember all the good experiences that she had with her cat. Although there will be pain and sadness and more crying when Sandy thinks of her pet, she is, as Dr. Balter describes it, coming to grips with the death of her cat. Eventually, when she finds Whisker's bowl behind the sofa, she decides to take it to school and give it to the class pet, a rabbit who needs a new bowl. Dr. Balter echoes Kübler-Ross' awareness that only when she has been allowed to express her feelings is Sandy "able to mourn successfully for her beloved pet and gradually move on to brighter days."

There are a number of fine books available that teachers and parents can use to help children understand about death and dying.

Let me share some of the books that I have used. I am confident that they will give the children what they need.

Wilhelm, H. (1985) *I'll always Love You*. New York: Crown.

This is a picture book about a boy's relationship with his dog, Elfie. The two have grown up together. When Elfie grows old and dies, the boy remembers that he has told his dog, "I'll always love you," each night at bedtime.

Warburg, S. S. (1969) *Growing Time*. Boston: Houghton Mifflin.

This book is appropriate for an older child (i.e., 7–10 years old). It has fewer pictures and is forty-four pages long. It could be read with a parent or by an older child alone. It describes Jamie's relationship with his dog King. When King dies Jamie has conversations with his grandmother and also with his Uncle John. They give him factual information about death and dying in a gentle and caring way. Both books should spark conversations with parents or caregivers.

Clifton, L. (1983) *Everett Anderson's Goodbye*. New York: Holt, Reinhart, and Winston

I highly recommend this picture book. It deals with the death of a parent. There are several things that make this book special. The illustrations are in black-and-white but the use of charcoal in the hands of a remarkable artist, Ann Grifalconi, has resulted in a work of art. This amazingly beautiful book is presented as poetry, simply expressed but greatly affective. The very first things described are Kübler-Ross' Five Steps of Grief. To review them, they are 1. Denial; 2. Anger; 3. Bargaining; 4. Depression; 5. Acceptance.

In his anger at his father's death, Everett Anderson says:

"I don't love Baby Evelyn

and I don't love Mr. Perry, too,

and I don't love Christmas or

Santa Claus

and I don't love candy

and I don't love you!"

But he moves through the five stages of grief and begins to heal as he remembers his father's love for him.

This lovely book has garnered many awards, among them the Coretta Scott King Award, was chosen as a Reading Rainbow selection, and an NCTE Teachers' Choice.

The four books described above all have similar approaches. They stress the value of talking and expressing the pain that is felt. This does not happen unless caring adults are there to listen, explain, and give hugs. The books that follow are recent discoveries. Although I have not used them in my classroom, they are quite wonderful:

Mellonie, B. and R. Ingpen. (1983) *Lifetimes: The Beautiful Way to Explain Death to Children.* New York: Bantam.

Brown, L. and M. Brown. (1996) *When Dinosaurs Die: A Guide to Understanding Death.* New York: Little Brown.

I particularly like this book because dinosaurs loom large in my kindergarten. I like my children to become experts on the varieties and characteristics of dinosaurs so they are a continuous source of study throughout the year. This marvelous book has a cartoon format with lots of information and cartoon characters expressing themselves, saying many of the things that children would say as an adult discusses this serious topic with them. In addition to a section on "ways to remember someone who dies," this book contains a discussion of what happens after death, according to various belief systems. This is fascinating material however, I think that an adult reader sharing the book with a child has some decisions to make about the amount of information to give. For example, if your family practices a particular religion, you might not be comfortable with the multicultural approach. While it is valuable for a child to understand that all around there are people who have differing beliefs, it might be helpful to point out, "This is what we believe."

Schwiebert, P. and C. De Klyen. (1999) *Tear Soup: A Recipe for Healing after Loss*. Portland, OR: Grief Watch.

This next book is unusual but may be just what is needed by some children. In it, an elderly lady, Grandy, prepares her "tear soup," and as she proceeds, the reader gets an idea of all the elements that cause her to grieve. The activity of making the soup and the memories that it calls up are valuable in helping her to deal with her loss. The book has several special features. It includes a computer address so that readers can send e-mails to a counseling service connected with the publisher, Grief Watch. Also there is a DVD available to be obtained online. I was surprised to find that there were a multitude of books available for all ages on this subject, so it is possible to find just the right book, at the correct level, to offer comfort.

13

Godzilla the Rat and Other Visitors

IT'S REALLY A DISGRACE! Parents send their precious children to school believing that they will thrive in the clean, secure environment that the Department of Education provides. Little do they know that as teachers we have to report accidents and crises to parents. For example, parents must be informed if there is a fire in the building, if there is an infestation of lice, if a child reports that abuse has occurred. But there are many events that may not be reported, outrageous things that are just weird and embarrassing.

The rodent problem, particularly on the first floor of an old building, never ends. When teachers return to school after summer vacation, their first task is "cleanup." I habitually bring rubber gloves, disinfectant, ammonia, sponges, and a pail. Although all classrooms have been cleaned at the beginning of the summer, by August the mice have again made their presence felt. All cupboards, closets, and shelves have to be disinfected again and regularly thereafter. Those little buggers are always waiting in the wings, ever ready to sabotage my program. One year we decided to grow flowers for Mother's Day. The children saved their milk cartons from lunch, and I washed them thoroughly. This was to be a "hands-on" spring project that involved science learning and the creation of a holiday present for mothers. The children enjoyed filling the cartons with soil, planting several seeds, and then adding water. As we placed the cartons on the windowsill, we reviewed the elements that plants need to grow—soil, sunlight, water, and air. We waited eagerly for the first green shoots, but nothing came up. Each day we checked the milk cartons. We didn't panic. I read them that charming little book, *The Carrot Seed*. When, for a long time, "nothing came up," after two weeks I panicked and planted a different seed mixture. But not one green leaf ever appeared. However, there were signs that the mice had discovered the seeds and had eaten them "all up."

I reported the rodent problem to the school custodian. However, I knew what to expect. Although the maintenance staff is generally thoughtful and helpful, my report about my Easter plants would not be viewed as a crisis. I got what I expected . . . several of those sticky mouse traps and a promise that when mice were caught in the traps, someone would come and remove them. When I shared my story with my principal, she informed me that every day at four o'clock a mouse left his hole and slowly crossed the room to another hole. She confided that she sat frozen in her chair until it was gone. She called the custodian. Traps were put down, but the mouse continued to visit.

No one wants to speculate about the size of the rodent population in New York. But we all know that it is in the zillions. Things are so bad that in all the parks and public places there are signs indicating where poison has been placed to control the rats. Well it isn't working. We are all aware of the seething masses in basements and under the sidewalks. Believe me, in the schools, even the littlest children think Mickey Mouse is cute, but scream in terror if they see a live one.

Because I live on the West Side of New York in a comfortable high-rise, I really never see mice. Garbage is sorted and recycled, the basement laundry rooms are spotless. We all seem to be "neat-niks," and yet sometimes something goes wrong and our worst nightmares come true. One evening, as I sat on my bed watching television, I heard a squeaking sound and a mouse ran across the room and disappeared under the love seat. I was so shocked that I screamed. Then I shuddered in disbelief as I remembered my friend's warning at lunchtime. Sarah, a second-grade teacher, who was very cynical but usually correct, had said, "Jean, Why do you always put your tote bag on the floor? You're going to be sorry . . ." In the precarious environment that is my classroom, the unthinkable had happened. I planned to throw away my tote and everything that was in it. But first I had to get rid of the mouse. I ran next door to the supermarket and bought two mouse traps (the sticky kind). All the time, I'm thinking, *It had to be in my tote bag.* It was conceivable that somehow a mouse had gotten into my grocery bag. However, I had not stopped at the store after school. The thought of that germ-ridden animal in my house, making a nest in the batting of my love seat was making me nauseous.

The sticky traps were at the base of my love seat. I waited nervously for the squeaks that would tell me that the mouse had been caught. Nothing! I slept with the light on that night. The room was quiet and in the morning the trap was empty. I scooted out of the room, showered, dressed, and left for school. I imagined the mouse coming out of his lair once I was gone and boldly walking around in my bedroom. Ugh! When I returned from school I quickly examined the traps. Nothing! Whereupon, thoroughly rattled, I called my mother. Mom, who probably had something on the stove, seemed a little annoyed with me. There are times when she gently admonishes me for not having "mother wit." This is the southern equivalent of "common sense." She said, and I quote, "Put some cheese in the trap." A half hour later the squeaking started. It was caught! I put on a glove, put the trap and the mouse in a paper bag, and dropped it down the incinerator chute. Ever since I learned that the fleas on rodents were responsible for the bubonic plague, my feelings about all rodents have hardened, so I have no feelings of remorse—only anxiety about the cleanup that awaited me. Sharks have a "feeding frenzy." I am capable of a "cleaning frenzy."

My last and most awful rodent story is a "must-tell" before I discuss how I decided to handle the mouse problem. My school is a big building. It was built to accommodate a larger population of children than exists in the area today. So that special programs are always being invited into the school. I was visiting the office workers of one such program when they began talking about their "rodent visitor." They were telling about a rat as big as a small dog or a full-grown cat. I was enthralled. It sounded like the equivalent of King Kong.

Every day at eleven forty-five a monstrous rat slowly walked across the floor of the room and disappeared into a closet. The first time they saw it, they screamed and screamed. But no one came so they jumped on top of desks and chairs. These women did not seem to be tellers of tall tales. They shuddered as they talked. The rat, whom I began to call Godzilla, had them truly terrified.

There were about four women in this office. Their program headquarters was off the playground and across from a huge construction site. The area was still Harlem, but was extremely valuable now, being gentrified, and becoming a community of town houses and upscale high-rises. In fact *all* of Manhattan had become extremely valuable real estate. However, there was another reason why Con Edison, construction companies, and the city were working so busily.

There are a number of underground streams flowing out of Central Park. I had learned that stately old Westside buildings have continuously flooded cellars because these streams cannot be controlled. It was not unusual for the platform of the nearby subway on 116th Street to be soaked and slippery from these streams. The frenzied rate of construction, where whole blocks of new housing were rising, the noisy laying of cables, wires, and pipes, were driving the rodents out of the subway tunnels, the cellars and sewers of the neighborhood, and specimens that had rarely been seen before were scampering around looking for new accommodations. This giant rat reminded me of the giant trout that fishermen whisper about. They survive because they are smarter and stronger than the other fish. The angler who catches one is stunned to find that the legendary "granddaddy" of them all is real. Well, Godzilla, the rat was on the scene now. According to the office workers, he didn't run across the floor; rather he strolled, expecting no interference. He was aware that they were afraid. He was not.

Several times I went to that office so I could see this phenomenon for myself, but was never able to stay long enough because I had to be back in my classroom, at the correct time, so that my covering teacher could leave. Godzilla's visits continued until the day that one of the ladies reported that he had appeared on schedule but was walking strangely. He was zigzagging and seemed confused. He wasn't strolling; he seemed to be dragging himself. Whenever I think of the next day, I shiver. An assistant teacher, on yard duty during lunch had come upon a kindergartener poking at something with a stick. On closer inspection she saw a huge body part of a dead animal. It was bloody and nasty and quite dead. The child was taken to the nurse where he was disinfected (just in case). It was not clear how much contact the curious child had had with the animal. Apparently this was the end of Godzilla, because he was never seen again. I would assume that the child's parent was informed but . . .

This disgusting tale leads me to talk tough about the rodent problem. Since I am writing this eight years later and the rodent problem has gotten no better (an assistant custodian remarked that at night there are so many rodents racing around the playground that it looks as if the ground is moving) I do what all sane educators do—ignore directives and use your judgment. Mice and rats avoid mothballs. However mothballs are poisonous so we may not use them. However, because I have had the experience of dying rodents interrupting my lessons and frightening my kids, actually dragging themselves across the floor in a dazed manner, and because I know that the fleas on rats were the real cause of bubonic plague in medieval Europe, I decided to go with the mothballs. My strategy was to choose inaccessible spots and salt them with mothballs. I sewed the mothballs into little net bags so that they wouldn't look like candy. Before the children returned in September, I had put mothballs behind the radiators, behind all the rolling bins, which the children never handle, in the teacher's coat closet and behind the teacher's desk, which is pushed up against the wall. Mothballs were never put in the children's closets or near their tables. A few were placed near stacks of paper on high shelves and in storage closets where children could not reach them. Since a cardinal rule is that the students are never allowed to be unsupervised in the classroom at any time, we were carefully watching to make sure that they did not encounter mothballs. However, the early socialization in September (the effort to acquaint them with their environment) includes a lesson about the mothballs (i.e., "If you see little white balls on the floor, or anywhere else, do not touch them. Call the teacher immediately. This is poison that we put down so that the mice stay away. Never touch mothballs. What should you do? . . . Call the teacher."

It works. I have never have had an incident. I never have mice in my classroom. Just remember . . . this lesson must be repeated whenever a new child enters your class. This is an example of "doing what cha gotta do" . . . to survive.

14

Relations with Support Personnel— Assistant Teachers, Guidance Counselors, and Special Services

WHEN I WAS WORKING in the Bronx at "The Country Club" as my elementary school was called, the children were generally well behaved. As I mentioned before, where a child was causing problems, it was easy to contact a parent and most importantly, see behavioral change. I always had large classes but the District Office Rule was that a teacher only got an educational assistant if the enrollment was thirty or above. When I had thirty-three students I got my first assistant, a lovely Italian lady, (the assistants were usually people from the community) who was a true treasure. Ed assistants usually are very artistic people so in addition to teaching, they love to beautify the classroom and do special art projects with the children. My Bronx assistant, a middle-class housewife whose children had gone off to private school, is still memorable for her good humor and delight in our daily schedule. She even liked doing yard duty during lunch and spent the time organizing circle games for the kindergarteners.

At my Harlem school with its disadvantaged population, educational assistants were different, and they had different roles to play.

At P.S. 207 our assistants were primarily there to help new teachers control difficult classrooms. Because I was what is called a "strong teacher" there were years where I did not have an assistant for the first six months. However, as increasing numbers of Hispanic children were coming into the school, many with no English skills, Hispanic assistants became necessary to ease this new population into the academic universe. At first the children were mainly of Puerto Rican descent, but soon there were a huge number of Dominican children. There were Bronx schools with eleven kindergartens. In fact I remember years where Hispanic students were being bused all over New York, and there was a need for more Hispanic teachers. Now, of course, at P.S. 207/149 we have African children, Hispanic, and Asian children. Because our neighborhood has housing provided for families where parents are completing drug rehabilitation programs, we occasionally have Caucasian children, too.

Class size is small now as we have gained recognition as a school with low reading scores. I am not sure what is happening now since my retirement, but policies of inclusion have brought many ADHD children into regular classes as well as unknown numbers of children born to drug-addicted parents, and indeed children who are HIV positive. We are never informed who is in this latter group, but all instructional staff is knowledgeable about the washing of hands, antiseptic packets to be used when children throw up, soil themselves, bite each other or the teacher. Under these circumstances, assistant teachers have an important role to play. Because the assistant is never supposed to manage the class alone, in emergencies she/he is the one who takes the child to the nurse or other professional staff. It is clear that with so many physically, emotionally, neurologically challenged children, the teacher and the educational assistant must function as a team. It is possible to have a successful and fun-filled year if as a team they like and respect each other. It is not wise to think of yourself as the professional and the ed assistant as the maid. You are sending a clear message if you are never seen sweeping or wiping up. There is a graciousness that we extend to our coworker that lets the person know that we are in this situation together and we will both do the things that make the program successful. For example:

1. The assistant is a valuable part of the academic program. Giving support during reading readiness lessons takes many forms. While the teacher is working with the class, the assistant may be working with one or two children who are not ready for the class lesson. Count on it. You will get a new child who has had no prekindergarten experience. The assistant can ease the new child into the program (i.e., teaching the new child to write his name, to learn classroom routines like "quiet reading" behaviors in the morning).

2. I do not let my assistant work on academic tasks until I have shown how alphabet letters should be printed, how homework sheets should be prepared, and how practice sheets should look. In this situation I am functioning as "the teacher as trainer." This is one of my most important duties. During preparation periods, I take the time, early in the year, to give the assistant teacher help in understanding our goals for the year, the reading program that has been selected by the school, and the ground that we will cover in our mathematics program. I dig out a sheet that has the letters of the alphabet so my partner can see how carefully printed letters should be constructed. I know that my children will be writing competently by spring so I want them to have superior handwriting. I model many behaviors for my educational assistant (i.e., to quiet a noisy class, I flick the lights . . . or I sing "Stop, Look, and Listen"). If my partner gets frantic and yells at a child, I try never to correct in front of the child. I write myself a note to speak about inappropriate language during lunchtime or naptime. I try to keep relations between us cordial, relaxed, and easy so the children see a united front. Let them see that we have standards and are in agreement about them; they can have a sense of security that they would not have if there was conflict between us.

3. Initially, I write all letters to parents; but gradually the assistant takes over this role. Frequently I will be asked to check a letter for spelling and grammar; sometimes the letter must be done over because letters with misspelled words and errors never go home. (Did I mention that neither the educational assistant nor the children can ever put anything on the bulletin boards that is misspelled? The children are so flattered to have work chosen for display that they patiently rewrite their work without protest.) To help my assistant achieve independence, I always keep a dictionary and a thesaurus in the classroom. We confer on grammatical usage where necessary.

4. Helping children to love the experience of learning, is a major goal of the year. A powerful way to do this is through the daily activity of storytelling. Generally, if children love stories, they have an interest in learning to read. Therefore we do everything possible to excite them with the joys of reading. The teacher and the educational assistant both need to be accomplished storytellers. The assistant will learn much by watching the teacher, but she must learn about the "art" of storytelling. Everything is important (i.e., how to hold the book; how to use your voice; how to explain unfamiliar concepts or words; introducing the children to the author, discussing the title page; how and when to ask questions). Discussions about these things should go on during preparation periods as the assistant chooses a story to tell the class. Also, the teacher should be there when the assistant tells a story so that praise can be given and gentle suggestions can be made. Storytelling is too important an activity to be handled in a hit-or-miss fashion. Both of the educators in the classroom should be able to stimulate hearts, minds, and imaginations.

5. The educational assistant always accompanies the class on all trips, neighborhood walks, trips to the community library. In preparation for trips the educational assistant

will be responsible for the identification tags that the children will wear, office papers detailing the trip (the principal must approve the trip); the kitchen must have notice and consult on food items for the children, and the bus company must have an official form signed by the principal before they will schedule a bus for the class. Frankly, I prefer to handle the first trip of the year, but after that the educational assistant takes over. This is a "modeling" situation. I model the behaviors that I want her/him to undertake.

6. The educational assistant handles many of the out-of-the-classroom tasks that must be performed. Written communications to the office, reports to the principal, attendance sheets, communications to the guidance staff (i.e., psychologist, social worker), relations with the library staff, other classrooms and teachers, all must be carried to the appropriate person or office. While I believe that monitors can carry attendance sheets to the office, private communications cannot be left to the children but must be transported by a responsible adult.

ASSISTANTS THAT I WOULD RATHER DO WITHOUT

a. We work very hard. Children must be picked up in the yard, taken to the lunchroom, escorted to library, gym, art class, to the toilet, wherever the class must go when the teacher has a conference, faculty meeting, or staff development sessions. In the classroom, we move from activity to activity. Occasionally, I find myself with an educational assistant who expects to spend the day in a sitting position. No chance! Even if the assistant is sitting and working with one student, it may be necessary to escort the child to the Word Wall to locate a word that the child will use in a story or the educational assistant will have to go to the bins to locate a book on the child's reading level. I also have "sitters" who like to color, decorate, and draw, and who resent being asked to do anything else. Such people don't last long in my classroom. Once I have explained my expectations, if things don't change, I am ready to negotiate a change. I often wonder how many miles I walk during a school day?

b. One year I had an educational assistant who resented taking orders. As egalitarian as I feel about us as a team, it is my job to plan and lead the academic program. I love to have an intern or educational assistant who is going to school and planning for a career as a teacher. I am proud to advise, critique, and suggest. But the responsibility for the success of the students is mine. We may plan together; if my assistant has ideas for lessons or experiences with the children, I am there to supervise, help with planning and evaluate in the most positive way. But one year I had an assistant who ignored my instructions, refused to follow my orders, and stood toe-to-toe with me, arguing and quarreling in front of the children. The principal clarified the situation. She said, "If I give a teacher a direct order and she refuses to comply I can write the teacher up as insubordinate; if the situation is serious enough, I can fire the teacher. If the teacher gives *you* a direct order and you refuse to comply, she could write it up, but you are being insubordinate and I can fire you." And lo and behold . . . the educational assistant became my best friend.

c. It is rare that an educational assistant comes with authority and immense skill in handling behavior problems. Yet this is an integral part of the job. We always have "acting-out" children, children who fight, children without impulse control. There are kindergarteners who will run out of the classroom, determined to leave school because they want to go home. Sometimes I will sit a crying child on my lap and wait for the weeping to stop. Sometimes I have to speak sternly and say, "We do not hit. We use words." "Youngster, you need a 'time-out.' Come with me. I want you to remain in the corner for ten minutes. I'll tell you when it's time to come back. You need to remember that those hands are for writing and drawing, but not for hitting!" Again, my assistant will watch the way I handle a crisis and learn. Sometimes I need to cajole. "Sharita, you need to finish that picture and write your name on it. But when you are finished, I need a monitor to get my black marker from my desk and bring it to the rug. Will you help me?" Or sometimes I am asking, "'Who's ready for a story? Whose legs are crossed? Whose eyes are on me? Whose hands are still?" It is important to know how to talk to small children. We must never belittle them or humiliate them. They respond to praise and good humor. I would not care to work with a person who makes fun of them or hurts their feelings. A really unkind thing to do is to compare a child to an older sibling that you have had previously. This is particularly painful to a child. "Your brother Johnny would never make a mess like this. He kept his portfolio neat with all the papers clipped together. What would he say if he saw your portfolio?" This is bad news. Comparisons with older siblings make children feel inadequate and unworthy. They become frustrated and very angry. Not good!

d. Assistants who are continually late or absent make my job so much harder. Being dependable counts! Working together we make the day go quickly. Working alone is fine as long as I expect to be alone. After I have planned the activities for the day and I learn that my assistant will be absent, I can quickly make adjustments. However, continual absence or lateness is unfair. The children are jolted because they respond to routines. They like to know what is coming next. They feel secure with predictable routines. When I have planned joint activities and my other half is not there, the program works less well. People with complicated romantic lives are not fun to work with. And while there are legitimate emergencies where a call via cell phone is acceptable and necessary, nonsense calls during the classroom day are unwelcome (you can tell each other how much you love each other during

lunchtime, but nobody interrupts my Morning Message).
It is really a question of dependability. A kindergarten
classroom runs really well when the teachers can depend on
each other. Otherwise, it gets messy. Some time ago I had
an unfortunate experience with an educational assistant
who was competent, well liked in our school community
and an "old timer" with many years on the job. The problem
was that she was all over the place. She could be found in
the kitchen helping the head cook prepare special meals or
she could be helping with the assembly program of another
educational assistant. She would say, "Just let me know
when you need me, and I'll be there." I have to say that
she kept her word and would return just as I was lining
the children up for toileting. She never understood that I
needed her there for one-on-one work with children having
problems. I needed her there when I was reading a story to
the class because I needed her to be sitting *with the children*
so that if Jason was poking Anthony, she could settle Jason
next to her and thereby prevent a tussle. In private we had
several bad moments when I tried to explain why I needed
her in the classroom with me because there were so many
things that she could do to make the day go more smoothly
(i.e., she could prepare the materials for the next activity).
She just ignored me. Eventually I told the principal that
her inability to give her complete attention to the classroom
was so upsetting to me that I would prefer to work alone. I
could manage my classroom perfectly well and she could be
deployed elsewhere. The principal actually removed her for
most of the spring term. I went on my merry way. She did
return to help with kindergarten graduation, but I made it
clear that she would not be my ed assistant next year. My
basic point is that a teacher needs to control her/his class. If
the teacher is new to the system and needs time to develop
skills in relation to discipline, an educational assistant is the
difference between chaos and walking off the job. But with

time, you get more skilled and as a senior teacher, you "run your own show." There is a wonderful sense of confidence and ease when you can do this. A good educational assistant has a million other things to do and she needs time to do them. An effective teacher can always control her students.

IN PRAISE OF DELORES

I take this moment to speak about the best educational assistant I ever had. In the fourteen years I spent at P.S. 207, we were together most of the time. Sometimes she was assigned to a new teacher or a new program for a year, but I always got her back. Delores Acevedo had qualities that made us a "dream team." For example, she was never late. Occasionally we would meet on the subway, but generally she was there before me. She was of Puerto Rican descent, and a grandmother. She had raised two daughters alone, and she was interested in working with me because she now had a granddaughter in prekindergarten, and she wanted to help prepare her for kindergarten. Her English skills were adequate or improving but she was so quick to ask questions, or able to listen carefully, so that there were rarely problems. She was good about checking with me to make sure that her printing was correct, or how she should reply to a parent's question. I became impressed with her ability to work with new children who did not speak English. She quickly developed a set of materials so that they could learn to write their names (a skill that thrilled them), and we took turns bringing them along in speaking English. (I think it is safe to say that a kindergartener who comes in to school in September with no English, will speak fluently by June. This is because young children are like sponges and soak up everything.) However, Delores would be working on writing skills also so they would make rapid progress.

Her computer skills proved to be a wonderful asset. For a few years we had a computer in the classroom. It took me years to control the stress that computers aroused in me. But Delores saw an area where she could make a difference. She found computer programs that reinforced the children's phonetic skills. She taught them to turn the machine on and even play phonic games with a buddy. I watched with amazement as she learned to create huge banner headlines for our bulletin boards and a birthday card for each child's special day. By springtime, some of the children were able to write stories of two and three lines by themselves, and Delores would print them out so parents could see their progress.

She was always able to add something to a project that gave it zing. I was preparing a display for our school fair that would show how well the children were writing. So I asked the children to write about their favorite story. To make it a showcase for critical thinking skills, I borrowed an idea from our curriculum guide and asked the children to identify the central problem of their favorite story. The children printed their responses on primer paper and drew pictures to illustrate their stories. I asked Delores to frame them; then we could put them up on the wall in the display area. She did a clever thing. The children who were not able to write a story got the chance to color the frames. Delores mounted the stories on poster board and made a three-inch border around the whole. When she divided the borders into triangles (like slanted capital *M*s) the children could color each triangle with a Magic Marker. The effect was bold and brilliant. I noticed that the colorful borders drew people to the display, and then they read the children's stories. It was a grand success. This wonderful educational assistant and I developed such literate children that at year's end, we took the class to the library and everybody who did not have one, got a library card. Because the library had a whole section of Easy Readers for early childhood, my children could come to the library all summer and read, read, read. Let me add that we met during the summer to evaluate the year and think about the coming semester in a West Side restaurant. And though I am retired . . . we still meet because we have become friends.

15

Intrinsic Intellectual Motivation: Its Relations to Social Class, Intelligence, and Achievement

IN LOOKING FOR BEHAVIOR that explained high academic achievement, we found a study that was so alluring that it led us to a thesis topic. In 1967, M. Gross did what no other researcher had attempted to do. He compared two subcultures within the religion of Judaism in a special way. He discovered that, when tested, children from these two subcultures showed differing achievement scores. These were preschoolers, and he was interested in their readiness to undertake academic work. One group, the Ashkenazim, Jewish children of central and eastern European background, achieved higher scores. The others were Sephardim, Jewish children of oriental backgrounds. All the children were from middle-class homes where English was the dominant language. When he discovered that there were differences in their performance on tests, he speculated as to the reasons why. He was aware that the children belonged to groups that had different cultural values. The Ashkenazim were a group who valued "love of learning" for its own sake, while the Sephardim were more instrumentally motivated toward specific goals (i.e., material gain).

The next step was to research the social science literature to find discussions of values like those of our two groups so that we could examine them in the larger school population and discover their effects on academic achievement. It was exciting to find that other social scientists had discussed similar value-orientations. We found several studies in which researchers showed interest in a motivation that has been called "love of learning." Alexander Meicklejohn (1969) had identified a predisposition or impulse that led some people to "delight in things intellectual" as worthwhile for their own sake. Crandall and Battle (1970) discussed adults who valued being bright, "verbally facile," and "knowledgeable" without relating these qualities to grades or academic competence. It seemed appropriate to call this motivation *intrinsic intellectual motivation* (IIM), an emotional response to the content and processes of intellectual learning. Those with this response (i.e., the Ashkenazim children) found learning activities immediately pleasurable. A contrasting impulse was found to be an instrumental motivation where there was no intrinsic impulse to pursue learning. Rather behavior served an ulterior goal. For example, the individual studies a subject in order to get a high grade but has no actual interest in the subject. This motivation had been discussed in several studies, but as a research variable its usage was vague and imprecise (i.e., it did not distinguish between intellectual and other tasks). In the literature it is called *need achievement.*

We decided to examine intrinsic intellectual motivation and need achievement to find out which social conditions influenced them. How were they related to academic achievement? What effect did social class, sex (gender), IQ have on IIM and need achievement, and how did they relate to academic performance?

The first step was to develop hypotheses. We needed to construct statements about the facts that we hoped to uncover and what we hoped to prove or disprove. These statements would assert that there were relationships between certain facts. Because this was a scientific investigation we had to test our hypotheses and either confirm them or reject them. But our hypotheses would not be random thoughts about the social world. They would be interrelated propositions (statements) that explained some aspect of reality and are what we define as a theory.

Hypothesis 1. There is a positive correlation between intrinsic intellectual motivation and academic achievement. Students who find learning activities immediately pleasurable—have intrinsic intellectual motivation—and will perform better in school.

Social class differences in child-rearing practices have been shown to produce differing intellectual and educational orientations (Davis and Havighurst, 1946; Ericson, 1947; Maccoby and Gibbs, 1954; Rosen and D'Andrade, 1959; Sewell, Haller, and Straus, 1957). Because of these social studies that relate social class to intellectual as well as educational development, a second hypothesis was suggested.

Hypothesis 2. There is a positive correlation between intrinsic intellectual motivation and social class.

The use of need achievement as an explanatory variable has created problems in the research literature. This is because it does not distinguish between motivation toward ends like power, status, or material gain from orientations to the task at hand. Nor is the distinction made between intellectual tasks and any other kind of task situation. While we acknowledge that both need achievement and intrinsic intellectual motivation are likely to influence a student's academic achievement, a goal of this research is to take into account the effects of need achievement when trying to parse out the effect of intrinsic intellectual motivation on achievement. We hypothesize that beyond the influence of need achievement, higher levels of intrinsic intellectual motivation will result in higher academic performance.

Hypothesis 3. There is a positive correlation between intrinsic intellectual motivation and academic achievement with need achievement controlled (semi-partialed).

There has been much discussion of intelligence and its relationship to educational mobility as well as social class. Significant correlations among these variables have been found. (Kahl, 1953; Sewell, Haller, and Straus, 1957) Recognizing the interrelationship of these variables, it seemed valuable to examine our variable of interest, intrinsic intellectual motivation for its relationship to achievement after the effects of intelligence are removed. A fourth hypothesis is proposed:

Hypothesis 4. There is a positive correlation between intrinsic intellectual motivation and academic achievement with IQ controlled (semi-partialed).

Finally, IIM's relationship to achievement is examined while all the relevant social and psychological variables are controlled. We expected to discover the influence of these variables as interrelating independent variables along with IIM on the dependent variable of academic achievement.

Hypothesis 5. Intrinsic intellectual motivation will have a positive effect on academic achievement with IQ, need achievement, and social class controlled (semi-partialed).

HOW WE GATHERED DATA

Our sample consisted of tenth graders (N=450; 274 females, 176 males) from two public high schools and one all-female parochial high school in New Jersey. Subjects were drawn as whole classes from the college-bound, middle-level track and vocational track in the public schools. In the parochial school, the entire tenth grade was used. Students responded to questions on three measuring instruments and filled out a survey about their social background. We used available data to get information about IQ and academic achievement.

   a. To measure a student's academic achievement, we used scores from reading tests from the high school battery of the Metropolitan Achievement Tests.

b. To measure social class, we used information from the Revised Occupational Scale for Rating Socioeconomic Status (SES). (Hamburger, 1968)

c. To measure need achievement we used the need achievement subtest of the Edwards Personal Preference Schedule (EPPS).

d. To measure IQ we made use of the available data in the school records. Tests used were the Lorge-Thorndike, the Henmon-Nelson and the Otis Beta. Scores were converted to standard scores based on national norms to allow comparisons to be made.

e. To measure intrinsic intellectual motivation we devised the Intrinsic Intellectual Motivation Scale (IIM), a questionnaire with forty-four questions. Here are some sample items:

  • When using the encyclopedia, I find myself reading articles that have nothing to do with the subjects I am looking up.

  • Teachers who take up time talking about things we are not going to be tested on annoy me.

  • College should help you get ahead, not just have you learn things.

METHOD OF ANALYSIS

To conduct our analysis we used Ordinary Least Squares regression analysis. This method allows us to measure the association between variables and to determine whether variables are positively related (as our hypotheses suggest). A complete discussion of the theories, method, analysis, and discussion of results (with tables and path analysis) can be found in the *Journal of Personality and Social Psychology*. (Lloyd. J. and L. Barenblatt, 1984)

SOME SIGNIFICANT RESULTS

The relationship between intrinsic intellectual motivation and achievement proves to be a strong one. We find that there is a correlation between the IIM scale and reading achievement of .37

(significant at the .001 level). Remember, anything that is significant at the .001 level is extremely important. Hypothesis 1 is confirmed.

The relationship between IIM and social class was expected to be a highly significant one. The data showed otherwise. The correlation between IIM and social class was low (.15) but significant. Hypothesis 2 was confirmed but the low correlation suggests that the influence of social class had been largely overestimated.

Our statistical analysis showed IIM and need achievement to be very different variables. The relationship (zero-order) between the two variables was negligible (.03). When we used a different method of analysis (stepwise regression) we attempted to test the relationship between academic achievement and the two variables, need achievement, and IIM. We found that need achievement accounts for 2% of the variance in academic achievement. When we add IIM it accounts for .13% of the variance not attributable to need achievement (at the .001 level). It is clear that by adding intrinsic intellectual motivation to our regression, we are able to explain more of the difference in academic scores between students. Hypothesis 3 is then confirmed.

The relation between IIM and IQ was of central interest to this research; the question was whether they possessed common features or attributes. The correlation matrix (Table 1) showed that indeed there was a relationship between these two variables (.27). This was significant at the .001 level. We could see that the relationship was not so great as to assume they were essentially the same. In a statistical analysis of academic achievement examining IQ and IIM (using stepwise regression) we find that the two variables alone account for 50% of the variance in reading achievement (see Table 3). The fact that IQ was entered first allowed it to soak up all the variance that it could. The resulting amount (46%) is no surprise because the relationship between IQ and achievement is well understood. But when we enter IIM into the equation and it accounts for an additional 3%, this amount is small but significant at the .001 level. This suggests that above and beyond IQ, a student's intrinsic intellectual motivation has an effect on test performance.

Hypothesis 2. There is a positive correlation between intrinsic intellectual motivation and social class.

The use of the need-achievement construct by theoreticians has created many problems. Usage of need to achieve as a construct and as a research variable has been vague and imprecise. The conceptualization of need achievement does not clearly distinguish between instrumentality toward further ends (such as power, status, or material gain) from orientations to the task at hand. Nor is the distinction made between intellectual tasks and any other kind of task situation.

Gross (1967) clarified the difference between such a goal-oriented, purposive motivation and a specifically intellectual and intrinsic motivation, when he speculated about the influence of subcultural values as he examined the Ashkenazic (Central and Eastern European) and Sephardic (Oriental) Jews. He guessed that the book centeredness of the Ashkenazim, who valued love of learning highly, accounted for their higher academic achievement than the Sephardim, a group equal in social class status as well as of similar religious affiliation, but a group stressing instrumental motivations related to need achievement. A goal of this research has been to determine the contributions of both motivations as they account for achievement and to explore the relations between them. This research then seeks to confirm the following hypothesis:

Hypothesis 3. There is a positive correlation between intrinsic intellectual motivation and academic achievement with need achievement controlled (semi-partialed).

The significant interrelationship of intelligence, educational mobility, and social class has been established (Kahl, 1953; Sewell, Haller, & Straus, 1957). This suggests that the main variable, IIM, be examined for its relationship to achievement where the effects of IQ are removed. The following hypothesis is therefore posed:

Hypothesis 4. There is a positive correlation between intrinsic intellectual motivation and academic achievement with IQ controlled (semi-partialed).

Finally, IIM's relationship to achievement is explored while the influence of relevant social structural and psychological variables are simultaneously controlled. We thought it necessary to ascertain the influence of these variables in their roles as interrelating independent variables along with IIM on the dependent variable of academic achievement:

Hypothesis 5. Intrinsic intellectual motivation will have a positive effect on academic achievement with IQ, need achievement, and social class controlled (semi-partialed).

Method

Sample

The sample consisted of 10th graders ($N = 450$; 274 females, 176 males) from two public high schools and one all-female parochial high school in New Jersey. Subjects were drawn as whole classes from the college-bound, middle-level track, and vocational track in the public high schools. In the parochial school, the entire 10th grade was used. Students responded to questions on three measuring instruments and filled out a questionnaire regarding social background. Administration occurred in two consecutive sittings arranged at the convenience of the pupils. Five of

Table 1

Correlation Matrix of the Variables in the Study

Variable	SES			Sex			EPPS			MAT			IQ		
	r	n	$p<$	r	n	$p<$	r	n	$p<$	r	n	$p<$	r	n	$p<$
Sex	−.01	399	.404	—	—	—									
EPPS	−.01	376	.431	−.29	417	.001	—	—	—						
MAT	−.30	391	.001	.12	405	.008	.15	384	.002	—	—	—			
IQ	−.30	365	.001	−.05	404	.161	.27	388	.001	.68	367	.001	—	—	—
IIM	−.15	400	.002	.22	445	.001	.03	422	.259	.37	406	.001	.27	408	.001

Note. SES = social class (socioeconomic status); EPPS = need achievement; IQ = intelligence; IIM = intrinsic intellectual motivation; MAT = Metropolitan Achievement Tests = academic achievement.

Table 2

Summary of Stepwise Regression Analysis: Dependent Variable—Academic Achievement; Independent Variables—Need Achievement and Intrinsic Intellectual Motivation (IIM)

Variable entered	Multiple R	R^2	ΔR^2	$F_{\Delta R^2}$	p	Beta
Need achievement	0.146	0.021	0.021	—	—	0.135
IIM	0.393	0.155	0.133	54.90	.001	0.365

the 455 were eliminated from the sample because they did not take the task seriously (e.g., refused to take the test).

Variables

Socioeconomic status (SES). This variable was measured by the Revised Occupational Scale for Rating Socioeconomic Status (Hamburger, 1968).

Need Achievement. This variable was measured by the need achievement subtest of the Edwards Personal Preference Schedule (EPPS).

IQ. The researchers made use of available data in the school records. Tests used were the Lorge-Thorndike, the Henmon-Nelson, and the Otis Beta. Scores were converted to standard scores based on national norms to allow comparisons to be made.

Intrinsic Intellectual Motivation Scale. The Intrinsic Intellectual Motivation Scale (IIM) is a Likert-like summated rating scale of 44 items. The following questions are sample items:

When using the encyclopedia, I find myself reading articles that have nothing to do with the subjects I am looking up.

Teachers who take up time talking about things we are not going to be tested on annoy me.

College should help you get ahead, not just have you learn things.

Cronbach alpha coefficients of internal consistency for the IIM Scale (Nunnally, 1972) were obtained from two samples of 10th grade students: .853 ($N = 100$) and .895 ($N = 100$).

Metropolitan Achievement Tests. Scholastic achievement was measured by the reading test from the High School Battery of the Metropolitan Achievement Tests

(Durost et al., 1964). It consists of three reading selections, each followed by questions testing comprehension and vocabulary.

Method of Analysis

The Statistical Package for the Social Sciences (SPSS) stepwise multiple regression (Nie, 1970) was used to evaluate the contributions of all the aforementioned variables to achievement-test scores.

Results

Zero-order correlations among the variables are given in Table 1. A correlation between the IIM scale and reading achievement of .37 ($p < .001$) was obtained confirming Hypothesis 1. (See Table 1.)

The relationship between IIM and social class was expected to be a strong one. The data showed otherwise (see Table 1). The zero-order correlation between IIM and social class was discovered to be low but significant ($r = .15, p < .002$). (The negative sign is an artifact of the numerical ordering of the values of SES.) Hypothesis 2 is regarded as being confirmed, but the low correlation suggested that although social class might have some influence on the development of IIM, its power as a causal factor had been largely overestimated.

Statistical analysis indicated that IIM and need achievement were indeed quite different

Table 3

Summary of Stepwise Regression Analysis: Dependent Variable—Academic Achievement; Independent Variables—IQ and Intrinsic Intellectual Motivation (IIM)

Variable entered	Multiple R	R^2	ΔR^2	$F_{\Delta R}^2$	p	Beta
IQ	0.681	0.464	0.464	—	—	0.627
IIM	0.707	0.500	0.036	24.244	.001	0.198

An examination of Beta coefficients clarifies this relationship even further. We compare Beta coefficients when the independent variables are measured in different units (if IQ is measured on a 100-point scale and IIM is the summary of a forty-four question survey the units of measure make comparison difficult). Beta coefficients standardize coefficients making analysis easier. Where a partial correlation was computed for IIM and achievement while controlling for IQ, the correlation was .260, significant at the .01 level. This means that when the effects of IQ are removed, the relationship holds. There is a positive correlation between IIM and achievement with IQ controlled *and* IIM accounts for almost one-third as much variance in achievement as does IQ. Hypothesis 4 is regarded as being confirmed.

Hypothesis 5 gives us a chance to look at the key variables (IQ, socioeconomic status, need achievement, and IIM), providing a powerful analysis of their effects on academic achievement. Using stepwise regression analysis the variables were entered based on theoretical understandings. (Table 4) It is important to note that the order of entry is significant here. If the first variable accounts for a substantial proportion of variance, new variables that are entered are not expected to effect change. IIM was entered last. The first variable entered was IQ. Its correlation with academic achievement was .681 and it accounts for 46% of the variance in achievement. The next variable entered was socioeconomic status. In the correlation matrix (Table 1) the relationship between SES and achievement is significant (-.30) at the .001 level. However the multiple regression analysis of Table 4 shows that SES has added an increment of only .010 to the explained variance in achievement. Of the four variables, the one making the least contribution to achievement is need achievement. While it has been shown to correlate with achievement (.15) significant at the .002 level, when it is combined with the variables IQ and SES it adds nothing to the explained variance and is statistically nonsignificant. Perhaps the explanation for this is that we need a better measurement tool. A better test might capture this variable and show a stronger relationship between need achievement and academic achievement. When we enter IIM into the regression analysis the strength of the IIM variable becomes apparent. Of the four independent variables examined in this equation, IIM is second only to IQ in the proportion of variance accounting for achievement. IIM was clearly a variable worthy of further exploration.

We first looked at sex or gender in relation to IIM. Was there a difference in the motivations to achieve of males and females? We highlighted the differences when we coded males=0; females=1. The direction of the zero-order correlations of Table 1 then became important. The relationship between sex and need achievement was -.29, significant at the .001 level. The relationship between sex and IIM was .22, significant at the .001 level. The positive direction of the correlation suggests that females were higher in IIM.

In the multiple regression equation when sex is entered first (Table 8), the correlation between sex and achievement is low .121, significant at the .008 level. Furthermore, sex accounts for 1 1/2% of the variance in the dependent variable, achievement. However, when IIM is added to the equation, together the two variables account for 14% of the variance in achievement and this is significant at the .001 level. Both the Betas and partial correlations also substantiate that it is not sex that is relevant here. The intruding variable of IIM makes the difference. The influence of the two variables together on achievement is .372. The semi-partial correlation between IIM and achievement with sex controlled is .354. When the influence of sex is removed statistically, the correlation between IIM and achievement remains.

Table 8

Summary of Stepwise Regression Analysis: Dependent Variable—Academic Achievement; Independent Variables—Sex and Intrinsic Intellectual Motivation (IIM)

Variable entered	Multiple R	R^2	ΔR^2	$F_{\Delta R^2}$	p	Beta
Sex	0.121	0.015	0.015	—	—	0.040
IIM	0.372	0.138	0.124	50.515	.001	0.361

fluence of sex is removed, the degree of relationship between IIM and need achievement is nonsignificant ($r_{43.5} = .103$, $p = ns$).

In the multiple regression equation when sex is entered first (see Table 8), the correlation between sex and achievement is low ($r = .121$, $p < .008$). Furthermore, sex accounts for 1½% of the variance in the dependent variable, achievement. However, when IIM is added to the equation, together the two variables account for 14% of the variance in achievement, and this is significant at the .001 level. Both the Betas and partial correlations also substantiate that it is not sex that is relevant here. The intruding variable of IIM makes the difference. The influence of the two variables together on achievement is .372. The semipartial correlation between IIM and achievement with sex controlled is .354. When the influence of sex is removed statistically, the correlation between IIM and achievement remains.

In the regression of IIM on IQ and SES, IQ accounts for 7½% of the variance in IIM, and the addition of SES proves to be statistically nonsignificant (see Table 9). This lack of significance and the low correlation between IIM and SES point to a noteworthy finding. These data offer the first inklings that the hypothesized positive correlation between IIM and SES may not hold. The previous evaluation of IIM

as a class-linked variable is now found to be spurious when the partial correlation (see Table 5) is examined. This correlation, which shows the relationship between IIM and SES when the influence of IQ is removed, is revealing ($r_{42.1} = .070$, $p = ns$). When IQ is controlled, the influence of SES on IIM disappears.

Path models, in terms of standardized regression coefficients may further illuminate the relationships around the variables under study. If we arrange the variables into three types: ascriptive variables (parental SES and sex), personality variables (need achievement, IIM, and IQ), and the outcome variable (academic achievement), we would see that the contribution of IIM to academic achievement (B = .162) takes place partly through the prior effects of sex (B = .222) and socioeconomic status (B = .144; see Figure 1).

However, it should be pointed out that there might be a confound in tracing the effects of sex, SES, and IIM on academic achievement, due to the disparate characteristics between public schools and the parochial school. A comparison of parochial and public schools as to results of the variables in the study is given in Table 10. A path model introduces the variable of public school/parochial school into the regression equation (see Figure 2).

In this path model, we see that there is a

Table 9

Summary of Stepwise Regression Analysis: Dependent Variable—Intrinsic Intellectual Motivation; Independent Variables—IQ and Socioeconomic Status (SES)

Variable entered	Multiple R	R^2	ΔR^2	$F_{\Delta R^2}$	p	Beta
IQ	0.274	0.075	0.075	—	—	0.252
SES	0.282	0.079	0.005	1.944	ns	0.071

Next we examined IIM as a dependent variable. We wanted to ascertain the contribution or complementariness of other variables to it. In the regression of IIM on IQ and SES, IQ accounts for 7 1/2% of the variance in IIM and the addition of SES proves to be statistically nonsignificant (Table 9). This lack of significance and the low correlation between IIM and SES point to a noteworthy finding. These data offer the first inklings that the hypothesized positive correlation between IIM and SES may not hold. Our previous evaluation of IIM as a class-linked variable is now found to be spurious when the partial correlation is examined (Table 5). This correlation, which shows the relationship between IIM and SES when the influence of IQ is removed, is revealing. When IQ is controlled, the influence of SES on IIM disappears.

Table 4

Summary of Stepwise Regression Analysis: Dependent Variable—Academic Achievement; Independent Variables—IQ, Socioeconomic Status (SES), Need Achievement, and Intrinsic Intellectual Motivation (IIM)

Variable entered	Multiple R	R^2	ΔR^2	$F_{\Delta R^2}$	p	Beta
IQ (standardized)	0.681	0.464	0.464	—	—	0.607
SES	0.687	0.474	0.010	7.635	.01	−0.091
Need achievement	0.689	0.475	0.001	0.625	ns	−0.022
IIM (Average)	0.713	0.508	0.033	25.120	.001	0.191

constructs. The zero-order correlation between need achievement and IIM was negligible ($r = .03$). In the multiple regression of academic achievement on IIM and need achievement (see Table 2), need achievement accounts for only 2% of the explained variance in scholastic achievement, whereas when IIM is entered it accounts for 13% of the variance not attributable to need achievement ($p < .001$). Hypothesis 3 is regarded as being confirmed.

The relationship between IIM and IQ was of central interest to this research; the question was the degree of commonality between them. The correlation matrix showed that, in fact, there was a relationship between these variables ($r = .27$, $p < .001$). However, the relationship was not so great as to assume that they were essentially components of the same construct. Tables 3 and 4 further clarify this relationship. Table 4 shows the combined effect of all four variables (IQ, need achievement, SES, and IIM), accounting for 51% of the variance in reading achievement scores. Table 3 shows that IQ and IIM alone account for 50% of the variance. Furthermore, IQ has been entered first in the equation so that it has the opportunity to explain all the variance that it can. Then IIM was entered and the increment $R^2 = .036$ was found to be significant at the .001 level.

An examination of Beta coefficients (see Table 3) shows that IIM accounts for almost one third as much variance in achievement as does IQ. This again demonstrates that there is something over and above IQ operating, and this is IIM. Partial correlations (see Table 5) also emphasize the theoretical separateness of these constructs. Where a partial correlation was computed for IIM and achievement while controlling for IQ, the correlation was .260 ($r_{64.1} = .260$). This was significant at the .01 level. There is a positive correlation between IIM and achievement, with IQ controlled. Hypothesis 4 is regarded as being confirmed.

Hypothesis 5 offered the chance to examine the effects of four pivotal variables (IQ, SES, need achievement, IIM) on the dependent variable, academic achievement. In the multiple regression equation (see Table 4) the variables were entered based on theoretical considerations that related to the variables of interest. Intelligence was the first of these. Its correlation with the criterion variable, academic achievement, was not unexpected ($r = .681$). The coefficient of determination shows that IQ accounts for 46% of the explained variance in achievement with a Beta coefficient of (.61). The next variable entered was SES. The zero-order correlation (see Table 1) for

Table 5

Partial Correlations of Interest

Partial correlation	r	df	p
First-order			
$r_{64.1}$	.260	364	.01
$r_{62.1}$	−.139	362	ns
$4_{64.3}$	.370	388	.001
$r_{61.2}$	−.265	362	.01
$r_{64.5}$	.354	402	.001
$r_{43.5}$	.103	414	ns
$r_{42.1}$	−.070	362	ns
Second-order			
$r_{64.12}$	.253	361	.02

Note. Variables are as follows: X_1 = IQ; X_2 = Socioeconomic status; X_3 = need achievement; X_4 = intrinsic intellectual motivation; X_5 = sex; and Y_6 = scholastic achievement.

DISCUSSION

A major implication of this study relates to educational policy making, particularly within public education. Since IIM correlates significantly with academic achievement, then a shift away from the present instrumental orientation may be in order. That the educational experience can be translated into higher lifetime earnings or higher social class may be less effective as an educational strategy than hitherto supposed. Because this orientation reflects the assumption that learning is a means to anticipated vocational and material rewards (the need achievement perspective), a commitment, instead, to the development of the intrinsic orientation, which makes the content and processes of learning a direct objective, offers a fresh orientation.

One of the hypotheses of this study was that IIM correlated with SES. Though this initially appeared true (Hypothesis 2), the regression of IIM on SES with IQ controlled showed the disappearance of the hypothesized relationship. This finding leads to a further inference. The theoretical assumption that the value orientations of differing socioeconomic groups as reflected in socialization practices and other "culture content" account for IIM has not been borne out by the data. New lines of inquiry must be opened in order to discover the sources of IIM.

Two major facts have emerged. First, IIM and IQ together account for the major amounts of variance in academic achievement in this study. Second, of all the variables examined, IIM is second only to IQ in the amount of variance for which it accounts. It is routinely accepted within the social sciences that IQ is a strong predictor of academic success. An implication of this study is that because IIM has been shown to be unrelated to social class, it may be helpful in predicting scholastic achievement across social class lines over and above the effects of IQ. If IIM can identify the students, regardless of social class, who have most to gain from academic stimulation, a related line of research should become the careful analysis of IIM to discover its dimensions (here only tentatively stated).

An additional finding of consequence has been the correlation between sex and IIM, females scoring higher than males. An implication of this study is that the socialization of males within this society pushes them in an instrumentally and vocationally oriented direction (as demonstrated by their higher need achievement), whereas the traditional socialization of females (in the role of transmitters of the culture) has encouraged the development of intellectual curiosity. It is ironic that the very qualities that are culturally acceptable in the fulfillment of domestic roles have influential contributions to make in educational attainment that in turn affect vocational attainment.

Further research might allow us to get at the specific school characteristics that produce an effect upon IIM. Among the possibilities are variables involving student selectivity, course content, intellectual climate, and teaching styles.

Jean Lloyd

Department of Sociology, University College

Rutgers University

Lloyd Barenblatt

Department of Organizational Studies

New York University

The preceding chapter is a discussion of the following article: "Intrinsic Intellectuality: Its Relations to Social Class, Intelligence, and Achievement."

Journal of Personality and Social Psychology

1984, vol. 46, no. 3: 646–654.

16

Templates for Arts and Crafts

I FIND MYSELF TAKING issue with the lack of emphasis on holidays that occurs in today's kindergartens. This is not a discussion about religion because holidays in America are secularized celebrations that all can enjoy. Thanksgiving, Frosty the Snowman, Halloween are all taken seriously by our children as they enjoy television, storybooks and movies. Attempts to offer alternatives to holiday celebrations overlook an important aspect of learning. We have a huge immigrant population in today's schools. Part of it consists of legal immigrants and part of it is made up of illegal immigrants. Because we do not deprive children of educational opportunities, our schools continue to accommodate children from around the world, many with little or no English skills. It is the function of our schools to socialize such children, to teach them English, but also about our country's history, institutions and culture. We must help them to absorb the values and customs of our nation so that they can function as intelligent citizens as they grow.

My Harlem school now has a stable population of Hispanic children (roughly twenty percent) and a rapidly growing population of African children from many different African countries. New York has rapidly growing groups of children from Eastern European countries, from Ireland and from many Asian countries. If we must educate these new Americans in our kindergartens the use of holidays has much value. Newly arrived children can learn much about our culture as they participate in its festivals. Please remember that this is very important to their parents, who want them to have access and realize the dreams that led them to leave other cultures and begin new lives in a vibrant society.

The curriculum surrounding holidays has been a traditional one in educational—institutions for generations and should be thought of as one of our "best practices" for integrating newcomers into our complex culture.

The objects found here are to be used as arts and crafts projects. They are curriculum supplements to units presented during classroom discussions and storybook experiences. They are mainly to be colored with crayons or markers and cut out using kindergarten scissors (metal without sharp pointed ends). Such activities are valuable in the kindergarten as children prepare to write. The manipulation of crayons, markers and scissors contribute to the strengthening of muscles of small hands that must practice writing alphabet letters and then words and finally sentences and stories. Kindergarteners love to color and go from random strokes to coloring within the lines, making decisions about which colors to use, and most importantly developing aesthetic satisfactions as they work. This is not meant to be "busy work."

Procedure: Use these templates to draw larger figures on heavy manila paper, the kind used for posters of office folders (filing). With a sturdy template the teacher can cut out the many copies that the children will use.

Always make extras as there will be do-overs.

Templates:

1. Figure Me: The teacher discusses the human body and guides the class in the placement of eyes, nose, mouth, hair,

tee-shirt and pants. Children use black crayons to draw body parts.

2. As summer turns to fall, discuss the color of summer leaves and the change to autumn colors (red, yellow or brown). I would indicate that this is a maple leaf which turns bright red.

3. Color pumpkin #1 after a trip to the pumpkin farm or grocery store. When coloring pumpkin #2, color the stem green, the eyes, nose and mouth yellow and the rest bright orange. They should be able to cut the pumpkin out following the black lines.

4. On candy cane #1 let the children make the stripes and cut out the object. On candy cane #2 the children can color the red stripes staying within the lines and cut out the figure.

5. I would have several templates available depending on the cultural interests of the class. The holiday tree is decorated with circles of different colors and glitter finishes it off. However, the teacher can make a Santa template and the children can add cotton to make a beard. Also, we have learned about Chanukah and made dreidels.

6. Valentines are fun to color and by February we can write messages to attach to the back (i.e., I love you).

7. The Easter bunny carries an egg in his paw with a message.

8. Mother's Day and Father's Day cards are fun to make and color. Messages to Mom and Dad (as appropriate, i.e. stepfathers, family friends) are written, then stapled on the back. Mom's card has a red rose and Dad's card is a shirt and a tie. The class could use markers to color these. Parents love to receive these tokens of their children's progress and affection.

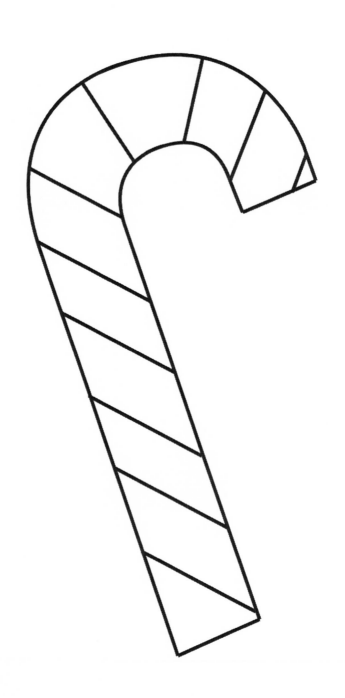

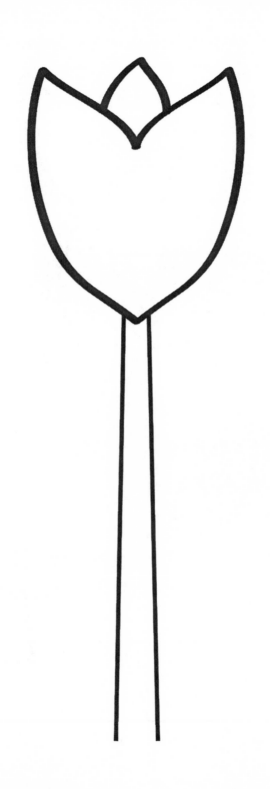

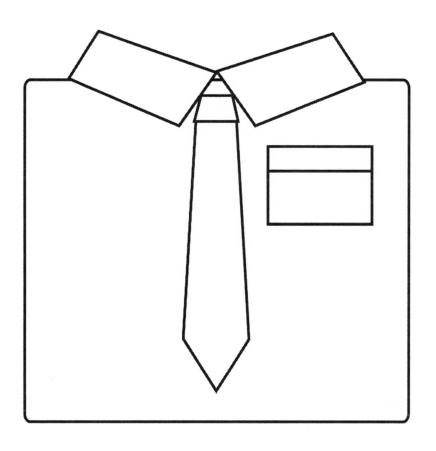

WHAT SYLVIA ASHTON-WARNER TAUGHT ME

SHE WAS MY INSPIRATION way back in 1984 when I left sociology and Rutgers University and returned to my first love, kindergarten. I loved her respect for her Maori children. She enjoyed their rambunctiousness, their honesty and their joy in making music. She lured children with no interest in literacy into writing about their fears, their troubled homes and the ghosts that were part of their tribal inheritance. She called the tough little boys her "warriors" and she rejoiced as they whirled through the first year of school, creating, listening to stories, singing and finally reading and writing, using her inspired system of giving them the words that had the most resonance to them.

However, when I had tried to implement her notion of "organic reading," I found myself in difficulty.

She was absolutely right about the intensity that words have for small children. They might not be able to read or write but their minds are like "volcanoes" bursting with energy and propelled toward creative or destructive expressions. Those interior pictures that she talked about (the neighbor's snarling dog, Mommy's kiss goodnight) were powerful representations and she believed a teacher need only give the child "captions" or words to illustrate these "mind pictures" to launch the child into reading and writing. Her method of giving the child words—writing down the words *dog* or *kiss*—was based on the realization that these were "key words" with power content so strong that once the teacher wrote the word and said it clearly, the child would remember it. She called them "one-look" words. Frankly, I had trouble implementing this piece.

My Harlem children did not remember the words that I gave them. I began to feel uneasy about an approach that reminded me of the "sight-say" method of my childhood, where we were supposed to learn words as whole units. I found that I felt more secure with a "phonics" approach because I believed that the child needed to be able to see the components that made up a word. If the word was "camp" the child needed to "sound out" the parts, then put them together to figure out the word. Ashton-Warner was committed to the "whole word" method that I learned as a child. It worked for me but then I had been quick and loved reading so it was easy. My little ones at P.S.68 needed to learn the sounds of the alphabet letters to give them the support to tackle new words. The American schools of education of the 1980s were also pushing the "whole language" method that focused on words as whole units. This approach was working in middle class schools but was having little success in schools like mine, where the children were disadvantaged. While I accepted the fact that the whole language method had worked with the Maoris (although I wasn't sure why it had not worked in Harlem) I began a phonics program, all the while feeling disloyal to my mentor Ashton-Warner.

Yet she was right about so many other things. She noted that when children are expressing themselves, there are no inappropriate words. They can talk about seeing grown-ups "drinking beer," or parents fighting. (Well, *she* says no inappropriate words but I exclude sex and cursing. I simply say that we don't use "that word" in school.) However, in principal, I agree that children should have the freedom to express themselves.

Sylvia Ashton-Warner is the only person I have encountered who understood about spelling. When she says, "Who can spell a word?" children pluck words from the store of key words because they are meaningful. It is true that little children can spell big words. Ashton-Warner says that words like "skeleton" have emotional value so they "get themselves spelled..."

I love that she stresses grammar and punctuation with little kids. This is a tricky area because correcting usage can cause some children to "clam up" for fear of saying or writing the wrong thing. And yet when gentleness and kindliness are practiced and respect is shown, it is possible to teach correct usage in kindergarten. For example, I have already commented that at attendance time, the child who is present must say, "I am here." This formal response is to coax them into speaking in grammatically correct sentences.

Since Ashton-Warner aims to move children from her "organic" reading program to the conventional European textbooks and she hopes to make the transition painlessly, a strict watch is kept on grammar and punctuation. While respecting the things that her Maoris bring, she must prepare them to succeed in the school system so that they can be productive adults.

And lastly, she has wisely allowed the children to teach each other. Once the children have collected their own word cards, they partner up and hear each other's words. "All of this, of course, takes time and involves noise and movement and personal relations and actual reading and above all communication, one with another: the vital thing so often cut off in a schoolroom."

And what present-day teacher doesn't use this technique, whether acknowledging Ashton-Warner or not? It is very noisy and chaotic when a roomful of children are teaching each other and it could explain the low ratings that she got when teacher performance was being evaluated but it was inspired and we recognize its effectiveness today.

BIBLIOGRAPHY

Ashton-Warner, S. (1959). *Spinster*. New York: Simon and Schuster.

———, (1963). *Teacher*. New York: Simon and Schuster.

Balter, L. (1991). *A Funeral for Whiskers: Understanding Death*. New York: Barron's Educational Series.

Beinstein, P. (2003). *Dora*. New York: Simon and Schuster.

Bemmelmans, L. (1939). *Madeline*. New York: Viking.

Karthwohl, D. and Bloom (1956). *Taxonomy of Educational Objectives: The Classification of Educational Goals*. New York: David McKay.

Bolton, F. et al. (1998). *Bookshop: Beanbag Books (Teacher's Resource Book, Stage 1)*. Greenvale, NY: Mondo Publishing.

Brooker, P. (2002). *A Glossary of Cultural Theory*. 2nd ed. New York: Bloomsbury USA.

Brown, Claude. (1965). *Manchild in the Promised Land*. New York: Macmillan.

Brown, L. and M. Brown. (1996). *When Dinosaurs Die: A Guide to Understanding Death*. New York: Little, Brown.

Bruner, J. S. (1963). *The Process of Education*. New York: Vintage.

Carpenter, S. (1998). *The Three Billy Goats Gruff*. New York: HarperCollins.

Comer, J. P. and A. F. Poussaint. (1975). *Black Child Care*. New York: Simon and Schuster.

Cooper, M. (1999). "Officers in Bronx Fire 41 shots, and an Unarmed Man is Killed." *The New York Times*, February 5, 1999, p.1.

Donaldson, A. G. (1985). "Management of Schools," unpublished paper. (Available from A. Donaldson, School of Education, City College, New York.)

Edgar, A. and P. Sedgwick. (2002). *Cultural Theory: The Key Thinkers*. New York: Routledge.

Dillon, S. (1993). "Elementary Schools Show Big Drop on Reading Tests." *The New York Times*, February 20, 1993, p. L22.

Freeman, D. (1968). *Corduroy*. New York: Viking.

Freeman, J. "Personal Sharing: My Whole Class Needed to Grieve." *Learning 91*. (March)

Grier, W. H., and P. M. Cobbs (1968). *Black Rage*. New York: Basic Books.

Gross, M. (1967). Learning Readiness in Two Jewish Groups: A Study in Cultural Deprivation, New York: Center for Urban Education.

Havill, J. (1986). *Jamaica's Find*. New York: Houghton Mifflin.

Herman, G. (1992). *The Puppy Who Went to School*. New York: Grosset and Dunlap.

Highet, G. (1950). *The Art of Teaching*. New York: Knopf.

Johnson, J. W. (ca. 1928). *Lift Every Voice and Sing: Quartette for Mixed Voices*. New York: Edward B. Marks.

Keats, E. J. (1962). *The Snowy Day*. New York: Viking.

Independent Readers (Winter Surprise, To Sam, Too many Toys, The Mitten) (1991). Geneva, IL: Houghton Mifflin.

Kraus, R. (2000). *Whose Mouse are You?* New York: Aladdin.

Kübler-Ross, E. (1997). *On Death and Dying*. New York: Scribner Classics.

Lewin, T. "Research Finds a High Rate of Expulsions in Preschool." *The New York Times*, May 17, 2005, p. A12.

Lindsay, V. (1929). The Little Turtle. In Pennell, M. E. and A. M. Cusak (eds.) *The Children's Own Readers (Book Two)*. New York: Ginn and Co. p. 123.

Lloyd, J., and L. Barenblatt. (1984). "Intrinsic Intellectuality: Its Relation to Social Class, Intelligence and Achievement. *Journal of Personality and Social Psychology*, vol. 46, no. 3: 646–654.

Maker, C. J. (1995). *Teaching Models in Education of the Gifted*. Austin, TX: Pro-Ed.

Mellonie, B. and R. Ingpen (1983). *Lifetimes: The Beautiful Way to Explain Death to Children*. New York: Bantam.

Milne, A. A. (1927). *Now We Are Six*. New York: Dutton.

Moore, C. C. (1936). "A Visit from St. Nicholas." In H. Felleman (Ed.) *The Best Loved Poems of the American People*. Garden City, NY: Doubleday.

Munsch, R. (1995). *Love You Forever*. New York: Firefly Books.

National Diffusion Network Project. (1987). *It's Time for Talents: Staff Development Manual*. New York: NYC Board of Education, Division of Curriculum and Instruction.

Postman, N. and C.Weingartner (1969). *Teaching as a Subversive Activity*. New York: Delacorte.

Schwiebert, P. and C. De Klyen (1999). *Tear Soup: A Recipe for Healing after Loss*. Portland, OR: Grief Watch.

Shuchman, M. "Psychological Help for Children in Urban Combat." *The New York Times*, February 21, 1991, pp. B9–10.

Snyder, Z. K. (1967). *The Egypt Game*. New York: Atheneum.

Steptoe, J. (1987). *Mufaro's Beautiful Daughters*. New York: Lothrop, Lee and Shepard.

Stoker, H. W. and R. P. Kropp (1964). "Measurement of Cognitive Processes." *Journal of Educational Measurement* 1, no. 1, 39–42.

Tommasini, A. "Franco Corelli: Italian Tenor of Power and Charisma, and Pillar of the Met, Dies at 82." *The New York Times*, October 30, 2003, C14.

Torrance, E. P. (1965). *Rewarding Creative Behavior*. Englewood Cliffs, NJ: Prentice-Hall.

———, (1974) *The Torrance Tests of Creative Thinking*. Lexington, MA: Ginn and Company.

———, (1979). *The Search for Satori and Creativity*. Buffalo, NY: Creative Educational Foundation.

U.S. Department of Education, Office of Educational Research and Improvement. (1993). *National Excellence: A Case for Developing America's Talent*. Washington, DC.

Wagstaff, J. M. (1999). *Teaching Reading and Writing with Word Walls*. New York: Scholastic Professional Books

Warburg, S. S. (1969). *Growing Time*. Boston, MA: Houghton Mifflin.

Wilhelm, H. (1985). *I'll Always Love You*. New York: Crown.

CPSIA information can be obtained at www.ICGtesting.com
Printed in the USA
LVOW042005260912

300452LV00001B/205/P